BS
Revelation

BEHOLD,
JESUS IS COMING!

JAIL MINISTRY

KAY ARTHUR
WITH DAVID ARTHUR

HARVEST HOUSE PUBLISHERS
Eugene, Oregon 97402

Cover illustration and interior art by Micha'el Washer

The International Inductive Study Series
BEHOLD, JESUS IS COMING!

Copyright ©1995 by Precept Ministries
Published by Harvest House Publishers
Eugene, Oregon 97402

ISBN 1-56507-318-5

Printed in the United States of America.

Contents

How to Get Started . . .

Reading directions is sometimes burdensome—often tedious! Sometimes you'd just like to get started. Only if all else fails will you read the instructions. I understand, but please don't approach this study that way. These brief instructions are a vital part of getting started on the right foot! These few pages will help you immensely. In fact, you'll probably be lost and frustrated in your study if you skip this section!

FIRST

First of all, let us explain how this study is set up. There is an assignment for every day of the week—so that you are in the Word consistently. If you work through your study daily, you will find it more profitable than doing a week's study in one sitting. Pacing yourself this way allows time for thinking through what you learn on a daily basis! In this study of Revelation you need to allot at least 28 minutes for study six days of the week for thirteen weeks.

The seventh day of each week has several features that are different than the other six days. These features are designed to aid group discussion; however, they are also profitable if you are studying this book individually.

The "seventh day" is whatever day in the week you choose to finish your week's study. On this day, you will find a verse or two for you to memorize and STORE IN

Your Heart. This will help you focus on a major truth or truths covered in your study that week.

To assist those using the material in a Sunday school class or a group Bible study, there are Optional Questions for Discussion. Read through these and then decide which ones you want to discuss in light of the time frame you have set. You will usually have more questions to discuss than you can cover in your weekly discussion time. Even if you are not doing this study with anyone else, it would be good for you to answer these questions.

If you are in a group, be sure every member of the class, including the teacher, supports his or her answers and insights from the Bible text itself. Then you will be handling the Word of God accurately. As you learn to see what the text says, the Bible explains itself.

Always examine your insights by carefully observing the text to see what it *says*. Then, before you decide what the passage of Scripture *means*, make sure you interpret it in light of its context. Scripture will never contradict Scripture. If it ever seems to contradict the rest of the Word of God, you can be certain that something is being taken out of context. If you come to a passage that is difficult to understand, reserve your interpretations for a time when you can study the passage in greater depth.

After the discussion questions is a Thought for the Week. In this study of Revelation many of these sections will be utilized to explain what we believe the Word teaches about future events. We by no means expect you to agree blindly with our stance. We do not believe we have a corner on the truth. Therefore, as you come to this section, have an ear to hear—be teachable, but discerning! As you consider our view, continue to study Scripture to see how what we believe lines up with what you see in the Word of God.

Remember, whether we agree on every point or not isn't the issue! Keep an open, teachable spirit! The issue is that you carefully observe the text for yourself! Learn to handle the Scriptures carefully and accurately by becoming familiar with the whole counsel of God.

SECOND

As you study Revelation, you will need four things in addition to this book:

1. A Bible that you are willing to mark in. The marking is essential. An ideal Bible for this purpose is *The International Inductive Study Bible (IISB)*. The IISB is in a single-column text format with larger, easy-to-read type, which is ideal for marking. The margins of the text are wide and blank for note-taking.

The IISB also has instructions for studying each book of the Bible, but it does not contain any commentary on the text, nor is it compiled from any theological stance. Its purpose is to teach you how to discern truth for yourself through the inductive method of study. (The various charts and maps that you will find in this study guide are taken from *The IISB*.)

Whatever Bible you use, just know you will need to mark in it, which brings me to the second item you will need. . . .

2. A fine-point, four-color ballpoint pen or various colored fine-point pens that you can use to write in your Bible. Office supply stores have these.

3. Colored pencils or an eight-color leaded Pentel pencil.

4. A composition notebook or a notebook for working on your assignments and recording your insights.

THIRD

1. As you study Revelation, your daily assignments will consist of various instructions that will help you see exactly what the Word of God says. These should take you between 25 and 30 minutes a day, but if you desire to spend more time than this you will increase your intimacy with the Word of God and the God of the Word.

Once you see what the Word says, then you can know how to interpret and apply it to your daily life. You may wonder how to do that. Well, that's why the International Inductive Study Series exists—to show you how to study book by book through the Bible until you see and begin to understand the whole counsel of the Word of God.

If you are doing this study within the framework of a class and find the lessons too heavy, simply do what you can. To do a little is better than to do nothing. Don't be an "all or nothing" person when it comes to Bible study.

Remember, any time you get into the Word of God, you enter into more intensive warfare with the enemy. Why? Every piece of the Christian's armor is related to the Word of God. And our one-and-only offensive weapon is the sword of the Spirit, which is the Word of God. The enemy wants you to have a dull sword. Don't cooperate! You don't have to!

2. As you read each chapter, train yourself to ask the "5 W's and an H": who, what, when, where, why, and how. Asking questions like these helps you see exactly what the Word of God is saying. When you interrogate the text with the 5 W's and an H, you ask questions like these:

a. **Who** are the main characters?

b. **What** is the chapter about?

c. **When** does this event or teaching take place?

d. **Where** does this happen?
e. **Why** is this being done or said?
f. **How** did it happen?

3. The "when" of events or teachings is very important and should be marked in an easily recognizable way in your Bible. I do this by putting a clock (like the one shown here) in the margin of my Bible beside the verse where the time phrase occurs. You may want to underline or color the references to time in one specific color. Some references to time that you will need to look for are: *coming quickly, done, finished, day, times, until,* and *forever.* Also mark any time references that give specific time frames such as: *forty-two months, time and times and half a time, day and night, one thousand two hundred and sixty days,* etc.

4. At various points in the study, you will be told to make lists, create charts, etc. Although such exercises may not be your favorite thing to do, following the easy and specific instructions related to each of these will grant you deeper and broader insight than you would gain without these exercises. Please understand that every instruction in this study has a purpose and know that following each will pay off!

5. You will be given certain key words to mark throughout the book of Revelation. This is the purpose of the colored pencils and the colored pen. If you develop the habit of marking your Bible in this way, it will make a significant difference in the effectiveness of your study and in how much you remember.

A **key word** is an important word that is used by the author repeatedly in order to convey his message to his reader. Certain key words will show up throughout the book; others will be concentrated in specific chapters or segments of the book. When you mark a key word, you should also mark its synonyms (words that mean the same thing in the context) and any pronouns (*he, his, she, her, it, we, they, us, our, you, their, them*) in the same way you marked the key word.

Marking words for easy identification can be done with colors or symbols or a combination of colors and symbols. However, colors are easier to distinguish than symbols. If I use symbols, I keep them very simple. For example, I color *repent* yellow but put a red diagram like this with it: **repent** The symbol conveys the meaning of the word.

When I mark the members of the Godhead (which I do not always mark), I color each word yellow. But I also use a purple pen and mark the Father with a triangle like this: **God**, symbolizing the Trinity. I mark the Son this way: **Jesus** and the Holy Spirit this way: **Spirit**

You should devise a color-coding system for marking key words throughout your Bible so that when you look at the pages of your Bible, you can see instantly where a key word is used.

When you start marking key words, it is easy to forget how you are marking them. I recommend cutting a three-by-five card in half lengthwise and writing the key words on that. Color-code the words on the bookmark in the same way you plan to mark them in your Bible. Then use the card as a bookmark as you work through the book under study. You may want to make one bookmark for words you are marking throughout your Bible and one for the specific book of the Bible you are studying.

6. A chart called REVELATION AT A GLANCE is located at the end of this study. As you complete your study of each chapter, record the main theme of that chapter under the appropriate chapter number. The main theme of a chapter is what the chapter deals with the most. It may be an event or a particular subject or teaching.

If you will fill out the REVELATION AT A GLANCE chart as you progress through the study, you will have a complete synopsis of the book when you finish. If you have an *International Inductive Study Bible*, you will find the same chart in your Bible. If you record your chapter themes there, you'll always have them for ready reference.

7. Always begin your study with prayer. As you do your part to handle the Word of God accurately, you must remember that the Bible is a divinely inspired book. The words that you are reading are truth, given to you by God so you can know Him and His ways more intimately. These truths are divinely revealed.

> For to us God revealed *them* through the Spirit; for the Spirit searches all things, even the depths of God. For who among men knows the *thoughts* of a man except the spirit of the man, which is in him? Even so the *thoughts* of God no one knows except the Spirit of God (1 Corinthians 2:10,11).

Therefore ask God to reveal His truth to you as He leads and guides you into all truth. He will, if you will ask.

8. Each day when you finish your lesson, meditate on what you saw. Ask your heavenly Father how you should live in light of the truths you have just studied. At times,

depending on how God has spoken to you through His
Word, you might even want to record these "Lessons for
Life" in the margin of your Bible next to the text you have
studied. Simply put "LFL" in the margin of your Bible,
and then, as briefly as possible, record the lesson for life
you want to remember.

Books in The International Inductive Study Series are
survey courses. If you want to do a more in-depth study
of a particular book of the Bible, we suggest you do a
Precept Upon Precept Bible study course on that book.
You may obtain more information on these courses by
filling out and mailing the response card in the back of
this book.

REVELATION

The Book of Revelation

Of all the books of the Bible, none has sparked more interest, curiosity, or disagreement than the book of Revelation. Of the 66 books comprising the Word of God, this is the one that promises a special blessing to the one who reads it and to those who hear and heed its words.

But how can we heed something we don't know or understand? Isn't the book of Revelation unknowable? Some people would say so. Others would advise you to stay away from it. After all, if the scholars cannot agree, how could ordinary laypeople expect to crack its mysteries!

We believe that behind all the mystery and controversy you will find one common foe—the serpent of old who is called the devil and Satan. After all, he holds the title of the "prince of this world." What a fool he would be not to do everything he could to discourage you from studying the book that so clearly shows the demise of his kingdom and the ultimate triumph of the One he so unjustly accused. What was lost—and has remained lost down through the millennia of the ages—when Adam and Eve listened to his lie is restored in the book of the Revelation. Revelation is the rest of the story!

The words of Revelation are faithful and true and, thus, worthy of our study, of our understanding. And understand you will if you exercise your spiritual senses to discern what the Lord says about the things which must shortly take place.

This inductive survey course will enable you to lay a solid and critical foundation. A foundation you can build on. A foundation that will stand and will hold you in the earthquakes and storms caused by every wind of doctrine and cunning craftiness of man. A foundation that will give you confidence in the face of controversy because you see for yourself "thus saith the Lord" about the things which must take place.

To really appreciate Revelation (and it is possible!), you should first study the book of Daniel in The International Inductive Study Series, *God's Blueprint for Bible Prophecy*. Daniel gives the big picture of prophecy, the general blueprint. Revelation fills in the details. So, consider working through Daniel first.

Unveiling the Future

As you work through this book we urge you to put aside all you have heard regarding the explanation of the book of Revelation. Come to this book with an innocent approach—no preconceived ideas. Simply see what the text is saying. Let the Word speak for itself. You will benefit greatly from the blessings that will come as you study Revelation inductively.

D<small>AY</small> O<small>NE</small>

Read through Revelation 1. As you read, look for who wrote the book and to whom it was written. You will find that time phrases are extremely important in the book of Revelation. We suggest that you mark every time phrase with the clock symbol as recommended in the "How to Get Started" section in this book. (You may also want to review the samples of time phrases listed for you in that section.) Or, of course, you could develop your own coding system. Refreshing your memory may help you as you begin so that you don't miss important phrases since they are so key to understanding!

Record your insights on who wrote Revelation and to whom it was written on the R<small>EVELATION AT A</small> G<small>LANCE</small> chart (page 141).

What did you see about those who read the book of Revelation? Are they blessed if they simply read the book? Read Revelation 22:7 also. Record your insights in your notebook.

DAY TWO

Read Revelation 1 again. You need to read this chapter several times because it contains much truth you'll want to absorb.

Now read Revelation 1:1,2 and think through how the author receives this revelation. What is it a revelation of? Watch your answer carefully. You are not looking for who gave the revelation but for what is going to be revealed. By the way, the Greek word for Revelation is *apokalupsis** which means "an unveiling." According to Revelation 1:1,2, what is going to be unveiled?

Now in your notebook draw a diagram/sketch which represents how this book came about. Think about the process and draw it—even if it is a rough sketch! You may feel like you aren't much of an artist and we understand! But believe us, sketching the process will help tremendously—even if you use stick figures!

In this first chapter the author was told to write three things. List these in your notebook and note the verse

---

* From time to time we will look at the definition of a word in the Greek. Since the New Testament was originally written in Koine Greek, sometimes it is helpful to go back to the Greek to see the original meaning of a word. There are many study tools to help you if you would like to do this type of digging. One excellent book to help you understand how to do more in-depth study is *How to Study Your Bible* (Harvest House Publishers, 1994).

where you find each one beside it. As you work through the book, you'll be making numerous lists of pertinent information. We suggest that you always note the chapter and verse where you find your insights beside each one as you list them for future references! When you go back to review your list, having the "address" of the insight will be most helpful! Also, since we suggest you list various insights in your notebook, you may want to think about how you'll organize your notes. One good way is to simply make notes by chapters— so you might want to divide your notebook into 22 sections and title each segment by chapter. Remember though, you'll have several lists that you'll maintain throughout the entire book, so leave a large section for such work.

DAY THREE

Before you begin today's work, make a bookmark on which you will record the key words and/or phrases that you will be asked to mark in chapters 1–3. Later you will make another bookmark to use in your study of chapters 4–22. Some of the words from the bookmark you make today will be transferred onto the bookmark for chapters 4–22 also, but most of the words will be concentrated in chapters 1–3. If you aren't sure how to make the bookmark, refer to the "How to Get Started" section at the beginning of this book.

Today we want to see what Revelation 1 says about Jesus Christ. Therefore, read the chapter and mark every reference to Him. Since you will also mark every reference to the Father and to the Spirit on days 4 and 5, if you do not have a particular way to mark the Father, Son, and Spirit, let us make a suggestion. Since all three are one in character and attributes, and since each are God, you might want to indicate their unity by using a triangle.

You could mark God the Father with a triangle like this: **God,** God the Son like this: **Jesus,** and God the Spirit like this: **Spirit.** So list these key words on your bookmark and color them there as you plan to mark them in your Bible.

Now, read the chapter and mark or color every reference to Jesus Christ. Don't miss any pronouns or synonyms which refer to Him. Remember, a synonym is a word or phrase that has the same meaning as another word and is used in the place of that word. For example, *son of man* is a synonym for Jesus. If you didn't read how to mark key words in the section "How to Get Started," stop now and read it so you understand how to best mark key words.

Mark any reference to the coming of Jesus Christ in another distinctive way. Make sure the references you mark are references to His return. As you study other books

of the Bible, you will want to mark any references to His
second coming in this same way so that you can always spot
these at a glance. (Because these references are so varied, we
can't give you all the specific phrases, but you'll see them!)

Read through Revelation 1 again carefully. This time examine the text in the light of the 5 W's and an H. Ask questions like: What do you learn about Jesus Christ? Who is He?
How is He described? Where is He? What is He doing?

DAY FOUR

Read through Revelation 1 and mark every reference
to God. Then in your notebook make a chart with three
headings: Jesus Christ, God, and the Holy Spirit. List
everything you learn about God from this chapter. Be
sure to leave several pages for the chart since you will add
to your list throughout the study. Remember to note the
chapter and verse beside each insight you record.

Now, add to your list all you learned from marking
references to Jesus on Day Three.

DAY FIVE

Read Revelation 1 again and this time mark every reference to the Spirit. Mark the reference to *seven Spirits* in
the same way you mark *Spirit*. Add this phrase to your
bookmark. When you finish, note all you learn about the
Spirit on your chart.

As you study Revelation and observe anything in the text
about any member of the Godhead, record it on your chart.

DAY SIX

What would you say is the theme of Revelation 1? (The theme is the subject that is dealt with the most in the chapter.) Record this theme on your REVELATION AT A GLANCE chart (page 141).

Go back and read Revelation 1:19 where you'll see that John is told to write three things:

1. "the things which you have seen"[1]
2. "the things which are"[2]
3. "the things which shall take place after these things"[3]

Now read Revelation 4:1. What do you see in this verse that relates to Revelation 1:19? Let's reason together. From what you observed, how would you divide the book of Revelation (by chapters) into the three parts listed above? Where does Revelation 1 fit? Where does Revelation 4:1 fit? Can you conclude where Revelation 2 and 3 fit in the structure of the book of Revelation? Record your insights next to the three phrases noting which chapter(s) correspond to each. This breakdown gives you the outline of the book of Revelation.

Now quickly read through Revelation 2 and 3 so you can see what these chapters are about.

DAY SEVEN

Store in your heart: Revelation 1:1-3,19.
Read and discuss: Revelation 1:1-3,9-20.

OPTIONAL QUESTIONS FOR DISCUSSION

ॐ From what you have learned just in Revelation 1, what is this book about?

ॐ Who is the book of Revelation for? Where is it to be sent? Give the details as to how the book of Revelation is given to the seven churches in Asia. As you discuss this, have the group share how they sketched the progression in Revelation 1:1,2.

ॐ How does the book of Revelation break down (or segment)? Or, to put it another way, what is John to write and how do the chapters of this book cover these three things?

ॐ What promise is connected with this book? On what basis? Do you think this promise applies to today, or did it only pertain to John's time? Why?

ॐ What do you learn about Jesus Christ from this chapter? Have the group refer to the chart in their notebooks.

ॐ Did you learn anything new about Jesus Christ? If so, what?

ॐ What do you learn about Jesus that might make a difference in:

    a. What you believe about Him?

    b. How you live now that you know what you do about Him?

    c. How you should pray?

    d. How you worship Him?

∾ What is the mystery of the seven golden lampstands and the seven stars? How do you know?

∾ Do you think we should study prophecy? Or is the study of prophecy just for scholars to debate? What is the benefit of prophecy? Look up and discuss Revelation 19:10.

THOUGHT FOR THE WEEK

Amos 3:7 says, "Surely the Lord GOD does nothing unless He reveals His secret counsel to His servants the prophets." God does not want to keep you in the dark regarding the future, beloved child of God. The future can be very scary if you don't know what is coming and who is in control. Thus, He has given you the Word of God and you will find in it the whole counsel of God, not only in regard to what you are to believe and how you are to live, but in respect to what the future holds.

It's all there in the Bible for you to know. Regardless of who you are or the degree of your education, if you are a true child of God you are indwelt by the Holy Spirit who is there to lead you and guide you into all truth. That He will do, if you will do your part. And what is your part? It is to read and heed the Word of God.

You are off to a good start, friend. Press on. Don't let anyone keep you from knowing and understanding the unveiling of the "things which must shortly take place" (Revelation 1:1). They are laid out for you in the book of Revelation. In chapter 1 John records the things which he saw as Jesus stood in His magnificence among the seven lampstands. Then, in chapters 2 and 3, John records the things which are: Jesus' message to the seven churches existing in Asia at the time of his writing. Finally from Revelation 4–22, John records for us what will take place after these things.

Study well and you won't be in the dark regarding the future and the things which must shortly take place!

WEEK TWO

What Happened to Your First Love?

DAY ONE

Read through Revelation 2 and note what John is instructed to do and to whom he is to do it. Add these words to your bookmark: *throne, repent, I know, deeds,*[4] *he who has an ear,*[5] and *let him hear what the Spirit says to the churches.*[6] Then mark all the key words or phrases listed on your bookmark. Don't forget to mark pronouns that refer to any of these key words.

DAY TWO

Since you are about to begin your study of Jesus' messages to "the seven churches that are in Asia," we will give you a brief description of each of these cities. Read the description of each city before you do the assignment which follows it. As you work, keep in mind what you read about each city.

Be sure to mark the salutation to each church, i.e., *to the angel of the church in . . . write.*[7] Mark each salutation in the same way. Mark, too, each promise to the overcomers, i.e., *to him who overcomes,* or *He who overcomes*[8] in the same way but in a distinct color from the salutation. Add

these phrases for the salutation and the promises to your bookmark.

As you read each passage pertaining to one of the seven churches, look for the following information and record what you learn regarding each church on the chart JESUS' MESSAGES TO THE CHURCHES on pages 47-51. (If this chart does not provide you with adequate space, create your own chart in your notebook.)

    a. Description of Jesus
    b. Commendation to the church
    c. Reproof given to the church
    d. Warnings and instructions to the church
    e. Promise to the overcomers

Now read the description of Ephesus. Then read Revelation 2:1-7 observing it according to the instructions above.

Ephesus

Because Ephesus was the chief port of Asia and on a key highway that led to several major cities, it was well-connected with the outside world. The port city was also the home of numerous Roman temples where many cults flourished. Not only was the church under continual pressure to conform to the idolatrous ways of these cults, it was also exposed to the influence of the world from the many visitors its accessible location and port activity drew in.

What has happened to Ephesus? What are they commanded to do?

What relationship do you see between the reproof and the promise to the overcomers. How do the two relate?

DAY THREE

Although you see Jesus threaten to remove Ephesus' lampstand, you will note as you study the other six churches that He does not threaten to remove their lampstands if they do not respond to His reproof.

Leaving one's first love must seriously and critically retard the purpose of the church. Therefore, look up the following verses and note what you learn that might pertain to your "first love" and what it means to leave your "first love." Watch for the word "love" and note what you learn about love from these passages. Record the verses and your insights in your notebook.

    a. Deuteronomy 30:15-20
    b. Mark 12:28-34

c. 1 John 5:1 (Note the relationship between loving God and loving others.)

d. 1 Corinthians 13:1-13 (Note the relationship of love to a person's works and gifts.)

e. Acts 2:41-47; 4:32-35 (Note what characterizes the lives of the believers. These references give an account of them right after they came to believe that Jesus was the Christ, the Son of God.)

Now, beloved child of God, take time to examine your relationship with the Lord in light of what you have learned. Have you left, or are you in danger of leaving, your first love? If so, you need to remember from where you have fallen, repent (have a change of mind that leads to a change of direction), and do the deeds you did at the first.

DAY FOUR

Smyrna

The city of Smyrna was so heavily dominated by Roman emperor worship that it was compulsory for every citizen to openly worship the emperor through the "voluntary" act of burning incense to Caesar. The immediate consequence for failing to comply with this mandate was death. Polycarp is a shining example of one who was faithful unto death as he was burned at the stake for refusing to deny his God by succumbing to man's law. The believers in Smyrna were under intense pressure to conform to their society.

Read Revelation 2:8-11 and mark the key words and phrases on your bookmark. Be sure to focus on all you see about the church in Smyrna. Refer to the list given in Day Two of all that you want to see as you study each church. Be sure not to miss the time phrase in 2:10.

Now, record your insights regarding the church in Smyrna on the chart, JESUS' MESSAGES TO THE CHURCHES (pages 47-51).

Think about the warning to this church regarding what is coming in the future. Also remember the promise of what awaits them if they remain faithful until death.

Was any reproof given to this church? Think about the reason. Do you know any churches in the world today that may be experiencing some of the same things the church at Smyrna endured? How would this message minister to them? Record your thoughts in your notebook.

DAY FIVE

Pergamum

Pergamum was not only considered an intellectual center since it was the first city of its day to erect a temple to an emperor of Rome, it was also perceived as progressive. Not only did the city boast a 200,000-plus volume library, second only to the enormous library in Alexandria, Pergamum was also home to the famous statue of Zeus which overlooked it. As a center for pagan worship and the administrative capital of the Roman province of Asia, people flocked to the festivals held at the temples and indulged in food offered to idols and sexual promiscuity. As the decadence of the city ate away at its core and as Satan's

stronghold grew, pressure to compromise and conform to
the worship of Roman and Greek deities weighed heavily
upon the church.

Revelation 2:12-17 records the message to the church
in Pergamum. Repeat the process you have been following in your study of the first two churches by marking the
key words and phrases from your bookmark and
filling in the chart JESUS' MESSAGES TO THE CHURCHES
(pages 47-51).

Do you see parallels between the problems in the
church at Pergamum and the state of churches in our
world? What do you learn from this message that you can
apply to the situation today?

DAY SIX

Thyatira

Thyatira was a city which boasted many skilled crafts-
men who comprised trade guilds. The power of the guilds
lay in their ability to forge the most beautiful and intricate
articles from brass and other materials and in the fact that
their work monopolized the market. Their items were
prominent in trade circles and were the centerpieces of much
of the idol worship in the pagan temples. Because of the
dominance the guilds enjoyed, the success of any individual
craftsman hinged on his becoming a part of such a group.
Since the guilds profited heavily from the sale of instruments
to the temples, they became extremely active
in idol worship. Since much of their livelihood hinged
on pagan worship, in order to protect their financial

well-being, the guilds focused great pressure on the church in efforts to sway them toward compromise.

Read Revelation 2:18-29. Mark key words and phrases and record any pertinent information on your chart, JESUS' MESSAGES TO THE CHURCHES.

In Pergamum there was *wrong teaching*. In Thyatira there was *toleration of a prophetess* (who was not only leading Jesus' bond-servants into immorality but was also eating things sacrificed to idols—the same two sins mentioned in the letter to Pergamum).

What do you learn from Jesus' message to this church about tolerating someone like this? Is this type of problem prevalent in any churches you know? What should the response of the church be in such an incident? Think about it and live accordingly.

Discern the theme of chapter 2 and record it on the REVELATION AT A GLANCE chart at the end of this book.

Don't forget to add any insights you've gained on God, the Spirit, and Jesus to your chart you began in Week One.

DAY SEVEN

 Store in your heart: Revelation 2:4,5.

Read and discuss: Revelation 2—one church at a time. However, if your discussion class is not long enough, discuss the church at Ephesus (2:1-7) and any other portion of the chapter that the Lord lays on your heart for your specific group.

Optional Questions for Discussion

∾ Why do you think Jesus closes each message to the churches with "He who has an ear, let him hear what the Spirit says to the churches"[9]?

   a. What does this closing tell you about each message? Is it for that specific church alone?

   b. Are each of these messages sent separately or are they contained in "one book"?

   c. Do you think Revelation 2 has a message for today's readers?

∾ Discuss what you recorded on the Jesus' Messages to the Churches chart in respect to each of the churches addressed in Revelation 2.

∾ What was the major problem with the church in Ephesus?

   a. How serious was the problem?

   b. What do you think it means to leave your "first love"? What do you learn from the Scriptures you looked up on Day Three?

   c. What is the cure for recovering your first love? How does this situation fit in with what you think it means to leave your first love?

∾ What do you learn about repentance and deeds from your study this week?

   a. Look at each occurrence of the word *deeds*[10] in chapter 2 and discuss what you observe.

   b. Look at each occurrence of the word *repent*. Does lack of repentance bring consequences?

ᔕ How has the Lord spoken to you personally in your study this week? Which message in particular stirred your heart? Why? What are you going to do in light of what He has said?

THOUGHT FOR THE WEEK

It is so easy to get into a routine of Christianity—serving the Lord . . . of duty until you lose the fervency, the sacrificial dedication of love. Christianity can become a performance without passion . . . and people can tell. And if people can tell, don't you know that Christ, the Lover of your soul, can tell?

Do you think He wants a perfunctory relationship or one of love? First Corinthians 13 makes it clear that if we do all the right things—even making the supreme sacrifice of giving our bodies in martyrdom for the kingdom of God—without passion, without the heart of love, then it is nothing in our Lover's eyes?

O Beloved, if love's fervor, love's sacrifice, love's obedience is diminishing or missing, you need to look back to see when it disappeared, why it disappeared, and do the deeds you did at first. Read Acts 2:42-47 and do what the early church did! Then watch the dying white embers of love blaze again into a brilliant consuming fire.

What If You're Not an Overcomer?

DAY ONE

Read through Revelation 3, marking the key words from your bookmark.

DAY TWO

Today we will continue looking at the seven churches.

Sardis

The chief city of Lydia, Sardis was located at the junction of the royal highways linking Ephesus, Pergamum, and Smyrna with the interior of Asia Minor and was situated above a valley among almost impregnable cliffs. In this location, as far as seven miles, the Necropolis, a famous cemetery known throughout the region, could be seen. The city was famous not only for its thriving dyeing and woolen industries but also for arts and crafts. Perhaps because Pactolus, a stream which flowed through the city, was a natural source of gold, Sardis became the first center to mint gold and silver coins. Its early prosperity became a byword for wealth. Although the city was protected from invasion by its natural surroundings, it was conquered in 546 B.C. by armies who scaled the cliff under the cover of darkness. The same tactics led to a second fall in 214 B.C. (The city had not learned from its past experience to be vigilant!)

Read the Lord's message to the church in Sardis in Revelation 3:1-6 and mark any key words from your bookmark you may have missed on Day One.

In the message to the church at Sardis, you will see the first mention of "white garments." You have not added this phrase to your bookmark because it is not used in chapters 1 and 2, but you should mark it in this chapter. Also mark the word *white* in 3:4 the same way you mark *white garments.*[11]

Since you will see several key words used in chapter 3 that will appear throughout chapters 4–22, why don't you stop and make your bookmark for those chapters now? On it put *white garments.*[12] You will need to mark synonyms for *white garments* too. No synonyms for the phrase appear in chapter 3 (other than the word *white*), but they do elsewhere so add these to your bookmark beside *white garments* and mark them the same way you mark *white garments.* The synonyms are: *white robe(s)* and *fine linen.*

Now, fill in the section for the church of Sardis on the chart, JESUS' MESSAGES TO THE CHURCHES (pages 47-51). Also note what you learn from Revelation 3:1-6 about *deeds.*

Be sure to note what you learn about *white garments.* Then ask yourself if your deeds are complete in the sight of God. Have you made a profession of faith but never carried through and lived out what you say you believe? Do you justly bear the name "Christian"?

DAY THREE

Philadelphia

Since the Greek word for love is *philadelphia*, it is believed that Philadelphia was perhaps named by its founder who chose this name for the city to commemorate his love for his brother. The district was an area of vine growing and wine production and, thus, a center for worship of Dionysus, the god of wine and fertility. Religious festivals and games were an integral part of the culture. The district sat on a broad, low, easily defended hill, but its location also made it subject to many natural disasters. One such disaster was the great earthquake of A.D. 17 which destroyed it completely. The city was well aware of the impermanence of life because of such disasters. And by the same token the church of Philadelphia was familiar with volatile, unstable conditions. Tiberius offered relief for the area, and the rebuilt city voluntarily assumed the new name of Neocaesarea.

Today we will look at the message to the church of Philadelphia in Revelation 3:7-13.

From this point on, there will be numerous references to *those who dwell (up)on the earth*[13] *(all who dwell on the earth, those who dwell in it)*,[14] so add this phrase and these synonyms to your bookmark. This group is mentioned only in Revelation, but mark these phrases throughout in a distinctive way so you can easily discern what this group is like and what will happen to them. This process will help you see why this group is distinguished in this book.

Note what the Philadelphia church is going to be kept from and why. Note everything you observe from the text about "the hour of testing"[15] and record it in your notebook.

Record your observations on the church of Philadelphia on the chart JESUS' MESSAGES TO THE CHURCHES (pages 47-51).

What column on the chart remains empty in regard to Philadelphia? Has this occurred with any other of the letters to the churches so far? Why do you think this is so for these churches?

DAY FOUR

Laodicea

The chief city of the wealthy province of Phrygia and situated on the major east-west trade route, Laodicea boasted a large number of banks. The city was widely known not only for its vast wealth but for clothes and carpets woven from the rich, glossy, black wool raised in its valley. The city was home too to a medical school which produced an eye salve. With all of its wealth and prominence the city lacked one vital resource—water. Water was piped to the area from hot springs much farther south and arrived lukewarm after traveling the distance in stone pipes. When destroyed by a devastating earthquake in A.D. 60, the city could afford to deny aid from Nero and reconstruct itself from its vast storehouse of wealth.

Revelation 3:14-22 contains the message to the last of the seven churches of Asia. Carefully read these verses, mark key words, and then record your insights on the JESUS' MESSAGES TO THE CHURCHES chart (pages 47-51).

As you read this letter, note all the parallels between what you know about this city historically and how those insights enhance your understanding of what our Lord says to this particular church.

What do you learn from this message about luke-warmness and the cure for it?

Identify and record the theme of Revelation 3 on your REVELATION AT A GLANCE chart.

DAY FIVE

How serious was our Lord's admonition and promise to the overcomers? How does it apply to our day? We want to explore these questions for the next two days. In order to answer these you need to review what you have seen in Revelation 2–3 and also look at chapter 21, plus consider a cross-reference in 1 John.

Remember that Scripture is the best interpreter of Scripture because the Word of God never contradicts itself. The Word explains itself as you consider all it says on a subject and thereby gain the full picture on the topic. As you look up cross-references in your studies, you may want to note the cross-references in the margin of your Bible next to the appropriate text in the book under observation. Cross-referencing helps you remember the location of a passage that sheds light on or correlates with the one you are studying. Cross-referencing is also very helpful when you don't have your study notes because your notes are right in your Bible!

Go back and look at every place you marked the phrase: *to him who overcomes* or *he who overcomes* in Revelation 2. Observe what you see in the text and record your insights on the chart, JESUS' PROMISE TO OVER-COMERS on page 43.

DAY SIX

Go through Revelation 3 today and follow the same procedure you did yesterday as you observed every occurrence of the phrase *he who overcomes*. Fill in the JESUS' PROMISE TO OVERCOMERS chart on page 43. Also look at Revelation 21:1-8 and write your insights in your notebook. Then, when you finish, look at what you've recorded. What are your observations thus far regarding overcomers?

Now consider 1 John 5:4,5 and record what you learn from this passage about overcomers on the bottom of the chart on page 43 under the heading WHAT 1 JOHN TEACHES ABOUT OVERCOMERS. Remember, both 1 John and Revelation were written by the apostle John. How does 1 John 5:4,5 compare with what you have seen about overcomers in Revelations? Think about it.

Maybe you thought that "overcomers" were an elite group of Christians and that a person can be a genuine Christian and not be an overcomer. From what you have observed this week, is this thinking accurate?

Don't lean on your own understanding; listen to and believe the Word of God. Think it through: If these are the

WHAT WE ARE TO OVERCOME	WHAT WE WILL RECEIVE IF WE OVERCOME	WHAT WE WILL MISS IF WE DO NOT OVERCOME

WHAT 1 JOHN TEACHES ABOUT OVERCOMERS

rewards of being an overcomer, then what would the consequences be of failing to be an overcomer? Can these consequences happen to those who are truly children of God?

Add to your chart begun in Week 1 any insights you've gained by marking references to God, Spirit, and Jesus.

DAY SEVEN

Store in your heart: Revelation 3:10 and/or 1 John 5:4,5.

Read and discuss: Revelation 3.

OPTIONAL QUESTIONS FOR DISCUSSION

∾ How would you describe the churches at Sardis, Philadelphia, and Laodicea?

∾ Discuss what you learned about each of the churches, including their strengths and/or weaknesses.

a. Look at each of the three churches you studied this week one by one. In your discussion, make sure you talk about what the Lord recommends for each one of these churches.

b. Can you relate in any way to one of these three churches? How? Why? What do you need to do?

∾ What two churches did not receive any words of reproof? Why do you think this was so?

∾ What church was not commended in any way? Why?

ᴥ What did you learn about overcomers? Are all true Christians overcomers or are only a select few? Have the group give a biblical basis for their answers. Keep asking, "What does the Word of God say?" and stick with that rather than using your own rationale. Discuss the consequences of not overcoming and, consequently, relinquishing the promises to overcomers.

ᴥ What is the most significant way God has spoken to you these past two weeks?

THOUGHT FOR THE WEEK

Beloved, you may have professed Christianity, but do you have the assurance that you possess Christ—that you have a relationship with Him and not just a religion about Him? Isn't it obvious from reading Revelation 2 and 3 that not all those who were connected with these churches were genuine believers? Not all were overcomers for "whatever is born of God overcomes the world; and this is the victory that has overcome the world—our faith. And who is the one who overcomes the world, but he who believes that Jesus is the Son of God?" (1 John 5:4,5).

Over a period of time, our works and lifestyles all bear testimony to the reality of what we profess. Yes, a child of God can sin, but a life of habitual sin, according to 1 John 3, shows that we are not children of God: "Little children, let no one deceive you; the one who practices righteousness is righteous, just as He is righteous; the one who practices sin is of the devil; for the devil has sinned from the beginning. The Son of God appeared for this purpose, that He might destroy the works of the devil. No one who is born of God practices sin, because His seed abides in him; and he cannot sin, because he is born of God. By this the children of God and the children of the devil are obvious: anyone who does not practice right-eousness is not of God, nor the one who does not love his brother" (verses 7-10).

Those who truly belong to Christ, who believe and abide in Him, are overcomers. They overcome the world because they believe God. O Beloved, hear what the Spirit is saying to you and do what He calls you to do. Jesus is coming and His reward is with Him. Listen and heed the words of the book of Revelation and you will be blessed.

	DESCRIPTION OF JESUS	COMMENDATION TO THE CHURCH	REPROOF GIVEN TO THE CHURCH	WARNINGS AND INSTRUCTIONS TO THE CHURCH	PROMISE TO THE OVERCOMERS
EPHESUS					
SMYRNA					

cont.

DESCRIPTION OF JESUS	COMMENDATION TO THE CHURCH	REPROOF GIVEN TO THE CHURCH	WARNINGS AND INSTRUCTIONS TO THE CHURCH	PROMISE TO THE OVERCOMERS

PERGAMUM

DESCRIPTION OF JESUS	COMMENDATION TO THE CHURCH	REPROOF GIVEN TO THE CHURCH	WARNINGS AND INSTRUCTIONS TO THE CHURCH	PROMISE TO THE OVERCOMERS

THYATIRA

cont.

	DESCRIPTION OF JESUS	COMMENDATION TO THE CHURCH	REPROOF GIVEN TO THE CHURCH	WARNINGS AND INSTRUCTIONS TO THE CHURCH	PROMISE TO THE OVERCOMERS
SARDIS					

	DESCRIPTION OF JESUS	COMMENDATION TO THE CHURCH	REPROOF GIVEN TO THE CHURCH	WARNINGS AND INSTRUCTIONS TO THE CHURCH	PROMISE TO THE OVERCOMERS
PHILADELPHIA					

cont.

	DESCRIPTION OF JESUS	COMMENDATION TO THE CHURCH	REPROOF GIVEN TO THE CHURCH	WARNINGS AND INSTRUCTIONS TO THE CHURCH	PROMISE TO THE OVERCOMERS
LAODICEA					

Do You Live As If He's Worthy?

DAY ONE

Today's goal is to get an overview of chapter 4. Read the chapter in light of the 5 W's and an H, asking questions like: Who are the main characters? What is happening? Where is it taking place? Also, consider again the significance of Revelation 4:1 in understanding the book of Revelation.

Don't miss the time phrase in Revelation 4:1. Draw a clock (or your symbol for time) in the margin of your Bible by the verse so that you note the phrase *after these things*.[16] Also write the reference "Revelation 1:19" in the margin next to this verse since Revelation 1:19 is crucial in understanding the structure of Revelation. Noting it here will help you keep the outline of the book before you.

DAY TWO

Read chapter 4 again, marking the key words on your bookmark for chapters 4–22. Also add to this bookmark *God, Spirit,* and *Jesus,* and remember to mark all references—including pronouns and synonyms—to the deity throughout chapters 4–22. Do not add words to the bookmark unless instructed to do so because it will become too difficult to use. We will continue to give you key words to mark that are specific to a chapter or portion of this book, but you don't need to add these to your bookmark. Today mark any occurrence of the word *worthy*. You will also see another mention of *seven Spirits*. Be sure to mark it as you did in chapters 1 and 3.

DAY THREE

Today read through Revelation 4 one last time. Mark every occurrence of the word *throne* and add it to your bookmark. Then, in a distinctive way, mark the phrase *immediately I was in the Spirit*.[17] References to John being in the Spirit or being carried away in the Spirit also occur in Revelation 1:10; 17:3; and 21:10. You have already marked *Spirit* in 1:10, but go back and mark the phrase *in the Spirit* there. Then take a moment and mark the other references just noted in the same way. Add any new insights to the list in your notebook on the Spirit.

In your notebook start a section where you will list the sequence of events of Revelation chapter by chapter from this point on. Title the section: THE EVENTS OF REVELATION.

Doing a concise synopsis of the events of every chapter of Revelation from chapters 4–22 will help cement the contents of the book in your mind. We'll refer to this list as our EVENTS LIST. Here's an example so you can see how to begin. Just think of the comprehensive list you'll have at the end of your study! What an overview of the book of Revelation you'll have!

The Events of Revelation

Location	Chapter	Events
(in heaven)	4	John is taken up and shown what must happen after these things. There he sees God's throne with the 24 elders sitting on 24 thrones. There are seven Spirits before the throne. Four living creatures are around the throne.
	5	All cry "Worthy" to God because He created all things and they exist because of His will.

By the way, did you notice all the worship in progress in chapter 4? This tells you volumes about heaven and about the priority there. Think about the contrast between what is happening in heaven with respect to God and what is happening on planet Earth with respect to the general attitude of people toward God. What a contrast!

DAY FOUR

Today, read Revelation 5. Observe this chapter in the light of the 5 W's and an H. Note who the main characters and people groups are, what they are doing, why they are doing what they are doing, and when events take place in relationship to one another.

In addition to the key words on your bookmark, mark the following words along with their pronouns: *the book*,[18] *worthy*, *Lamb* (Jesus), and *seven Spirits* (mark this phrase as you have before).

DAY FIVE

Read through Revelation 4 and 5 and add any new insights to your list on God and Jesus. Then make a list of all you observe about each of the key words you marked in these chapters.

DAY SIX

Today review what you learned this week from observing Revelation 4 and 5 by asking yourself the following questions to see how much you can remember of what you've studied.

+ Where do the events of these chapters take place?
+ What do you learn about this place? How is it described?
+ Who is on the throne? Before the throne? Around the throne?

* What is taking place? Why?
* Who is worthy? Why?
* What do the four living creatures look like?
* What is in the hand of the One on the throne? How is it described?
* Why is John weeping?
* How is the Lamb described?
* Why is the Lamb worthy?
* How do the 24 elders worship Him?
* What do you learn about those purchased by the Lamb?
* What is in the golden bowls?

Now check your insights against the text.

Add the events of Revelation 5 to the EVENTS LIST you started in your notebook. Remember to keep it simple! The events of Revelation will take you from earth to heaven, to the abyss, to the bottomless pit, so make sure you note where the various events begin, end, or take place.

Identify and record the themes of Revelation 4 and 5 on your REVELATION AT A GLANCE chart.

DAY SEVEN

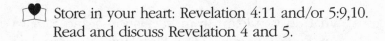 Store in your heart: Revelation 4:11 and/or 5:9,10. Read and discuss Revelation 4 and 5.

OPTIONAL QUESTIONS FOR DISCUSSION

~ How does Revelation 4 fit into what the Lord instructed John to write as stated in Revelation 1:19?

∾ How would you describe the events in Revelation 4 and 5?

   a. What do you learn about heaven from these chapters? What is it like there? What is happening? Who is involved?

   b. What do you learn about God and the relationship of the Spirit and the Son to the throne of God?

   c. What do you learn about the four living creatures and the 24 elders?

   d. Why is God praised as worthy in Revelation 4?

∾ What is in God's hand in Revelation 5? How is it described?

∾ What causes John to weep?

∾ What do you learn about the Lamb from Revelation 5?

   a. How is the Lamb described?

   b. Why is the Lamb worthy to open the book? (Get your answer straight from the text.) In what verse do you find your answer?

   c. What do you learn about those who are purchased by the blood of the Lamb?

   d. What is in the golden bowls that are before the throne? What does this tell you about the value of prayer?

∾ What do you learn from Revelation 4 and 5 that you can apply to your own life? How do you live in respect to what you have learned about the Lamb from Revelation 5?

THOUGHT FOR THE WEEK

Those who are around the throne, who see God and the Lamb as they really are, cannot help but cry, "Worthy! Worthy! Worthy!" They understand. They know for a surety that it is God who created them—and everything else. They know that all that exists, exists because God brought it into being. It exists because this is what God desired.

O Beloved, do you realize that the reason you exist, the reason you are alive, is because this is what God willed? You are an expression of the will, the pleasure, the desire of God!

And—although like each of us, you once lived in sin;

although you lived for your own pleasures rather than God's;

although you walked according to the prince of the power of the air, the spirit that works in the sons of disobedience;

although you were overcome by the one who deceived Eve in the garden of Eden, you have a kinsman-redeemer!

You have the Lion of the Tribe of Judah, the One who left heaven and took upon Himself the likeness of man, so that He might redeem you from the kingdom of darkness.

You have been purchased by the blood of the Lamb of God, the only Lamb ever slain who could take away your sin.

You have been made a kingdom, priests unto God; you will reign upon the earth.

Someday, maybe sooner than you think, the Lamb who has overcome will take the book, break its seals, and thoroughly redeem all that we lost in Adam and Eve when they chose to believe the father of lies rather than God. The Lamb of God will get back for you, His kinsman, what was forfeited in Adam—the title deed to the earth.

Never fear, dear friend. God has not—nor will He ever—leave His throne! He will reign forever and ever! Soon the mystery of God will be finished as He takes His great power and begins to reign visibly through His Son.

It is all coming! It is as sure as the promises of God. How then are you, beloved of God, to live in light of this? You are to live in such a way as to lay power, riches, wisdom, might, honor, glory, and blessing at the feet of the Ones who alone are worthy of such things.

O Beloved, take stock of your heart, your passions, your goals, your ambitions, your energies. Is the way you order your days, your life, worthy of the name you bear—Christian? For whose pleasure do you live? How do you live in respect to the One whom you call Father?

Remember you belong to a new kingdom—His kingdom. You are a priest unto God! Live in such a way that your life testifies of your priestly calling. Present your sacrifice—yourself. It's not an unreasonable thing to do in the light of who God is and why He brought you into being!

Someday you will reign with Him! Now is the time to prepare for that day. Instead of living in submission to the dictates of a world and society that is soon to be judged by our righteous God, live as more than a conqueror through

Him who loves you and gave Himself for you. Remember whose you are and therefore who you are.

Persevere! Remember what is going to take place and occupy in faith until He comes. Your heavenly Bridegroom is preparing your place. He will come again. Even so, come quickly, Lord Jesus, come!

The Breaking
of the Seals

DAY ONE

Read Revelation 6. In addition to marking the key words on your bookmark, mark every occurrence of the word *seal(s)* in a distinctive color or way. In the margin of your Bible number the seals as they are mentioned so you can easily locate them.

Now go back to Revelation 5 and mark every occurrence of the words *seals* and *sealed*. Is there any connection between Revelation 5 and 6 in respect to the seals? How does what happens in Revelation 6 line up chronologically with Revelation 1–3? Also remember Revelation 4:1. Record any insights in your notebook.

DAY TWO

Read Revelation 6:1-8. As you observe these verses, ask the 5 W's and an H. Note who the characters are, what they are doing, and what happens as a result. Stick with what the text says. Don't try to identify the characters at this point. List everything you observe about the first four seals in the appropriate space on the chart THE SEVEN SEALS, TRUMPETS, AND BOWLS (page 140).

DAY THREE

Read Revelation 6:9-17 and list everything you observe about the fifth and sixth seals on the chart THE SEVEN SEALS, TRUMPETS, AND BOWLS. Mark the word *wrath*[19] and add it to your bookmark.

DAY FOUR

Read Revelation 7 and mark the key words from your bookmark. Also watch and mark any occurrence of the word *seal(ed)*. Note any references to time and mark these. You will see a reference to robes—*washed their robes and made them white*. Be sure to mark this reference as you have been marking *white robes*.

In Revelation 7:1-8 you saw a group numbering 144,000 mentioned. Examine this group in light of the 5 W's and an H. Note who they are, where they come from, where they are, what happens to them, why, and when.

DAY FIVE

Read Revelation 7:9-17. Mark any occurrence of the word *tribulation*. Examine the group of people mentioned here in light of the 5 W's and an H. As you observe this group, note where they are, who they are, where they come from, what they are wearing, what they are saying, what their future is, etc.

DAY SIX

Review the content of Revelation 6 and 7. Put the events of these chapters on your EVENTS LIST. Remember to keep your descriptions brief.

Add any insights you may have gained on God and Jesus (the Lamb) to your notebook list.

Record the themes for Revelation 6 and 7 on the REVELATION AT A GLANCE chart.

DAY SEVEN

Store in your heart: Revelation 7:15-17.
Read and discuss: Revelation 6.

OPTIONAL QUESTIONS FOR DISCUSSION

❧ Have the class take out their EVENTS LIST. See if they can state the themes of Revelation 4–6. List these themes on the board. Then ask them to describe the first six seals. Then, allowing the class to refer to THE SEVEN SEALS, TRUMPETS, AND BOWLS chart, list what happens when each of the six seals is broken.

❧ Ask: What prompts each rider? Who is opening the seals? Who is in control?

❧ Discuss what they learn about each of the first five seals.

❧ What happens when the sixth seal is broken?

a. Note exactly what happens to the sun, the moon, and the stars.

b. How do the people react?

c. Who are the people who react this way?

d. What is said about the great day of wrath? Who says it?

∾ What two large groups of people are mentioned in chapter 7?

a. What do you learn about the large group mentioned in Revelation 7:4?

b. Why are they sealed? Is there any indication of when they are sealed?

∾ What do we learn about the second large group?

a. Who are they and where are they?

b. What do you know about them? How are they clothed? Why?

c. What are they saying? What are they doing?

d. What is their future? What does their future indicate about their past? Note where they come *out* from.

THOUGHT FOR THE WEEK

Although the four riders of the Apocalypse have captured the imagination of man, how many people stop to ponder who it is that releases these riders and brings forth these terrible events upon the earth?

Some have said that the rider of the white horse is Christ Himself, yet careful observation of the text shows us that Jesus is not the one on the horse but the One in heaven breaking one seal after another of the seven-sealed book. And with the breaking of every seal, we see the effect on mankind. It is not a pretty picture, but it is one which will be painted by the hand of our righteous God on the soiled canvas of the earth.

And what of God's people—the Jews—and all the other people who wash their robes in the blood of the Lamb? God does not leave us in the dark. He tells us that, before any further judgments come which will harm the earth, the sea, and the trees, He will seal 144,000 Jews from the twelve tribes. He also tells us that in addition to those martyred and heard from at the fifth seal, there will be others who will wash their robes in the blood of the Lamb. In the time of the great tribulation, there will be another group who in the midst of the judgments, will embrace the Lamb in faith and, thus, wash their robes in His blood and make them white, even as some in Sardis were clothed in white. God has a remnant and in the midst of His wrath He remembers mercy. He sends forth an angel to proclaim the everlasting gospel to those who live on the earth—to every nation, tribe, tongue, and people—calling them to fear God, to give Him glory, to worship Him (Revelation 14:6,7).

If you hold to a literal interpretation of the Word of God, it is obvious that this account is yet to take place. However, as we study, we must ask you, Beloved, where you stand in respect to the Lamb of God. You have been studying Revelation for the last five weeks. You have read and observed the first seven chapters of this sure word of prophecy. The words you have read in the book of Revelation are "'faithful and true'; and the Lord, the God of the spirits of the prophets, sent His angel to show to

His bond-servants the things which must shortly take place" (Revelation 22:6). He says, "I am coming quickly" (Revelation 22:7). Once the process begins, once the scroll is taken from the hand of God and the seals are broken by the Lion who is the Lamb, the events of Revelation will transpire quickly. An avalanche of judgments will be poured out and nothing will stop them. Where will you be on that day? Secure in Christ, clothed in white—or caught in the wrath and judgment of God?

What have you done with Jesus Christ? What do you believe about Him? If you have a faith that overcomes the world, then you are secure in the fold of God. But if not, friend, then you have not known true salvation, and you need to repent—to have a change of mind that will cause you to believe that Jesus is the Christ, the Son of God. Then you will know the victory that overcomes the world!

Now is the hour to examine yourself to see if you are really in the faith—now, before "the hour of testing, that hour which is about to come upon the whole world, to test those who dwell upon the earth" (Revelation 3:10).

Write out your confidence or your decision in your notebook. Put it in black and white.

The Trumpets Are Blown— Woe, Woe, Woe

DAY ONE

This week you'll observe Revelation 8, 9, and 10. Remember, the objective in this study is accurate observation of the text. Our goal is to take a fresh, unbiased look at the book of Revelation.

Today read Revelation 8. In this chapter you are introduced to the *trumpet(s)*, which is a new key word. Mark it in a distinctive way. You also need to mark the words *blasts*[20] and *sound(ed)* since these are used often in reference to the trumpets. (These words are used throughout chapters 8–11 in conjunction with the trumpets, so mark them as you mark the word *trumpet*. However, when you mark *sound*, make sure you mark only those references which refer to the *trumpet* sounding.) When you mark any of these words, note the number of the trumpet in the margin of your Bible. Also note each mention of a trumpet. Remember to mark any reference to the word *seal*.

Before you read, so that you can mark them consistently throughout the rest of Revelation, add the following key words to your bookmark: *thunder*,[21] *lightning*,[22] and *woe(s)*.

When you mark the word *woe(s)*, always note what the woes are connected to. Also mark any time phrases connected with them. This will help you understand the chronology (time sequence) of the woes.

DAY TWO

Read Revelation 8 again. Record your insights on the seventh seal and on the first four trumpets on the chart THE SEVEN SEALS, TRUMPETS, AND BOWLS (page 140).

DAY THREE

Read Revelation 9. Mark the key words from your bookmark and continue to mark any references to the trumpets. Remember to mark the words listed on Day One that relate to trumpets. Do not miss marking *repent* as you marked it in chapters 2 and 3. Also, carefully observe and mark all references to time because these indicate the sequence, timing, and duration of events.

DAY FOUR

Read Revelation 9 again. Add the information on the fifth and sixth trumpets to the chart THE SEVEN SEALS, TRUMPETS, AND BOWLS (page 140).

DAY FIVE

Add any insights on God to your list. Also, record all

the events of Revelation 8 and 9 on your EVENTS LIST.
Record the themes of these chapters on the REVELATION
AT A GLANCE chart (page 141).

DAY SIX

Read Revelation 10 and mark the key words from your
bookmark. Then record what happens in this chapter on
the EVENTS LIST. Add any new insights to your notebook
list on God. Also record the theme of Revelation 10 on
the REVELATION AT A GLANCE chart.

DAY SEVEN

Store in your heart: Revelation 9:20,21.
Read and discuss: Revelation 8:13–9:21.

OPTIONAL QUESTIONS FOR DISCUSSION

ॐ What happens when the seventh seal is broken?

ॐ Where in Revelation 8 is there a record of thunder,
lightning, and an earthquake?

ॐ As you look at THE SEVEN SEALS, TRUMPETS, AND
BOWLS chart, what happens when each of the six
trumpets is blown?

ॐ What do you learn from marking the word *woe(s)* in
Revelation 8 and 9?

a. When is the first woe?

b. When is the second woe?

c. When are the first two woes complete?

∞ How do the first six trumpets compare with the first six seals? Are they one and the same, or are they different? How do you know?

∞ Is anyone in control of all these events? Who? Support your answer using Scripture.

∞ What is going to happen when the seventh trumpet is blown?

∞ What do you learn from Revelation 9:18-21 about the state of mankind?

a. What is their response to these plagues?

b. When you marked the word *repent*, what did they *not* repent of?

c. What does this action—or lack of it—tell you about the state of mankind during this period of time?

THOUGHT FOR THE WEEK

If you take the book of Revelation literally and let it speak for itself, without adding your own interpretation or saying that it is all symbolic, then it is obvious that the events described for us in Revelation 6–22 have not yet occurred.

You also see that the cataclysmic events are not just "Mother Nature" gone crazy. Rather, these events are judgments coming from heaven to earth. The seals are different from the trumpets, and it seems that one judgment follows another because Revelation 9:12 says, "The first woe is past; behold, two woes are still coming *after* these things." And Revelation 10:7 says that when the seventh angel is about to sound the mystery of God is finished. There also seems to be a progression of intensity in these judgments since the events that occur after the trumpets have sounded seem worse than those that occur after the seals are broken. When the seventh seal is opened, the trumpets begin. It appears that the seventh seal contained the trumpets. Watch and see what happens with the seventh trumpet—we study that next week!

In all of this, do you see man broken by these judgments and turning to God en masse? No. After the sixth trumpet sounds bringing plagues of fire, smoke, and brimstone, and killing a third of mankind, people still do not repent. They continue in their idolatry and worship of demons. Murders, sorceries, immorality, and thefts continue. Those who still dwell on the earth get a small taste of hell, and yet do not seek to wash their robes in the blood of the Lamb.

What about you, Beloved? Has the goodness of God led you to a genuine repentance? Have you had a real change of mind as to who God is and His sovereign right to rule over you as your Lord, your God? If not, repent before Jesus takes the book and breaks its seals and unleashes the just judgment of God upon this earth!

If you already know God, Beloved, are you warning people to flee from the wrath which is sure to come upon the earth? You were saved to serve God, and one of the ways you serve Him and His kingdom is by being His witness—proclaiming His Word in season and out of season, using it to reprove, rebuke, and exhort with longsuffering and sound teaching. Share what you are learning!

When Satan Is Cast Down to Earth

DAY ONE

Well, Beloved, you've now observed the breaking of the seven seals and the blowing of six of the trumpets. Now let's move into an examination of Revelation 11 and 12 to see what they tell us about the things which happen "after these things" as recorded in Revelation 4:1.

Are you beginning to see why observing and writing down the events in Revelation helps you to better grasp the events of Revelation and their relationship to one another? As you read Revelation 11 and 12, it's critical for you to observe all references to time and anything that shows you how one event relates to another.

Remember to let Scripture speak for itself, to take it in its single literal sense. Yet at the same time be careful to respect the nuances of grammar and to appreciate the writer's use of figures of speech.

Today read Revelation 11 very carefully. Mark key words from your bookmark. Also mark references to the trumpets. Mark the word *nations*[23] and add it to your bookmark. Also mark every reference to the two witnesses, including any synonyms and pronouns which refer to them. In your notebook make a list of everything you see about these two witnesses. As always, remember to ask questions using the 5 W's and an H in your observations:

a. What do the two witnesses do?
b. How long do they do it?
c. Who does it affect?
d. What is their relationship to the beast?
e. According to the text, where does the beast come from?
f. Where do the two witnesses get the power to do what they do?
g. What happens to them? What city is being referred to in Revelation 11:8?
h. What is their final state? How does it come about?

Don't forget to mark the time phrases. When you mark the time phrases note any event that happens. (Remember that the Jewish calendar has 360 days instead of 365. Therefore 42 months and 1260 days are two ways of saying the same amount of time: 3½ years.)

When you finish reading Revelation 11, mark the word *beast* in 11:7 and add it to your bookmark. This is the first occurrence of *beast* in Revelation, but it will become a key word from this point on. Also mark *make war* (*wage war*, any reference to *war* including going to or having a war[24]) and add this key phrase and its synonyms to your bookmark.

DAY TWO

Read Revelation 11:1-13 again and mark the word

temple. When you finish reading and marking this word, note what you learn by listing them in your notebook.

Now read Revelation 11:14-19. In verse 14 observe what is said about the woes. Note which woe is past and which one is coming. When God interjects the fact that a certain woe is now past, ask yourself why He says it at that particular point in the book of Revelation. Everything has a purpose! Therefore, it may be that God is showing us the time of the woe in relationship to the events just recorded in Revelation 11:1-13. Think about it.

On the chart THE SEVEN SEALS, TRUMPETS, AND BOWLS (page 140), record what happens when the seventh trumpet is sounded by the angel.

Compare the seventh angel sounding in Revelation 11:15 with Revelation 10:7. Note what Revelation 10:7 says is finished with the sounding of the seventh angel. Mark these verses as cross-references to one another in your Bible: in the margin beside Revelation 10:7 write Revelation 11:15-19, and next to Revelation 11:15, write "Mystery of God Finished, Rev. 10:7."

You have already marked the word *wrath* since it's on your bookmark. Observe whose wrath comes, when it comes, and who is saying it has come. This is the third mention of the word *wrath*.

DAY THREE

Read Revelation 12 to get an overview. This chapter is loaded with valuable information and needs to be read and reread. Mark any key words from your bookmark. References to time will be key, so don't miss them. Remember the phrase "time and times and half a time" is the Jewish way of saying 3½ years.

Also mark every reference to the *woman* including pronouns. Mark every reference to the *dragon* including all synonyms (i.e., *serpent, Satan, devil*) and pronouns. Add the word *dragon* and its synonyms to your bookmark.

Now examine what you learn about the dragon from this chapter and make a list in your notebook of everything you observe about him. Note how he is described, who he really is, what his relationship is to the woman, what happens to him, when it happens, how he is overcome, what happens when he is cast out of heaven, what effect it has on the earth, how long he has after he is cast out, and what he does to the woman when he is cast out.

DAY FOUR

Read Revelation 12 again. Make sure you've marked every reference to the *woman*. Also mark every reference to the woman's *child*.

When you finish, list everything you learn about the woman in your notebook. Note how the woman is described when she flees into the wilderness and why she runs. Note the relationship chronologically to the birth of the woman's son and her flight into the wilderness. Reviewing the phrases will help. List, too, all you learn about the son. Mark the word *wilderness*[25] in this chapter. Compare the verses with others where you marked *wilderness*.

Also watch for references to time.

If you have questions as to the identity of the woman, stop and think about all you've observed from the text about her and about her son. Think about what you learn about the woman's male child because it is a clue as to the identity of the woman. Who is to rule all nations with a rod of iron? (You may want to look at Revelation 19:15.) Where is He now? When He was born were there any attempts on His life? By whom? What was his human heritage? (What nation was He born into? What people did His mother belong to?)

If you have time, you might enjoy reading Genesis 37:9-11 to see if you note any similarity between this passage and the description of the woman in Revelation 12:1. Remember that Jacob is the father of the twelve tribes of Israel. Note who is bowing down to whom in this dream. Don't be confused by this comparison of Scripture—just take what you can see at the first reading.

DAY FIVE

Read Revelation 12:1-6 and list in your notebook the order of events in this segment. Drawing a timeline using stick figures will help you see the progress of events. Now, carefully read through Revelation 12:7-17 and observe what happens when there is a war in heaven. Then look at how the word "now" in verse 10 relates to the "and when"[26] in verse 13.

Finally, you may want to distinctively color the phrase *was thrown down*[27] or *has been thrown down*[28] in Revelation 12:9,10, and 13. Then draw a line from the phrase in verse 9 to the word *now* in 12:10. Then draw the line from *now* to *and when the dragon saw that he was thrown down* in 12:13. With your Bible marked in this way your eye can easily see how these verses relate to one another "time wise." (See the example below.)

12:9 And the great dragon was thrown down, the serpent of old who is called the devil and Satan, who deceives the whole world; he was thrown down to the earth, and his angels were thrown down with him.

12:10 And I heard a loud voice in heaven, saying, "Now the salvation, and the power, and the kingdom of our God and the authority of His Christ have come, for the accuser of our brethren has been thrown down, who accuses them before our God day and night.

12:13 And when the dragon saw that he was thrown down to the earth, he persecuted the woman who gave birth to the male child.

You have marked the references to the woman and to the wilderness, now note the parallels between Revelation 12:6 and 12:14. Do you think these references are to the same period of time or to different incidents? Could it be that God gives the big picture in Revelation 12:1-6 of the woman and the dragon, and then in Revelation 12:7-17 fills in the details by repeating part of the account of the woman?

DAY SIX

Read through Revelation 12 one last time; then compare Revelation 12:10 with Revelation 11:15-17. Do you see any parallels that might indicate a chronological relationship between the seventh trumpet and the time when Satan is thrown down to earth and persecutes the woman for 3½ years? If you think there is a parallel, you may want to mark these cross-references in your Bible.

Record the main events you observed in Revelation 11 and 12 on your EVENTS LIST.

Add to your notebook list any insights on God and Jesus.

Record the themes of Revelation 11 and 12 on your REVELATION AT A GLANCE chart.

DAY SEVEN

Store in your heart: Revelation 11:15-17.
Read and discuss: Revelation 11:14-19 and 12:7-17.

OPTIONAL QUESTIONS FOR DISCUSSION

∞ What happens when the seventh trumpet sounds?

    a. Discuss what is said when it sounds, what happens, and how the nations respond.

    b. Discuss the timing of the seventh trumpet.

    c. When are you told the second woe (sixth trumpet) is past?

    d. From observing the text, how do you think the second woe relates to the events recorded in Revelation 11:1-13. Why?

∞ What is the relationship between the seventh trumpet

and the mystery of God? What do you learn about the mystery of God in Revelation 10:5-7?

∾ What do you learn about the two witnesses from Revelation 11?

   a. What do they do?

   b. How long do they do it?

   c. Who does it affect?

   d. What is their relationship to the beast?

   e. According to the text, where does the beast come from?

   f. Where do the two witnesses get the power to do what they do?

   g. What happens to them? What city is being referred to in 11:8?

   h. What is their final state? How does it come about?

∾ From what you observed about the woman in Revelation 12:1, who do you think she represents? How does Joseph's dream in Genesis 37:9-11 relate to the woman or give you insight into her identity?

   a. What does the text tell you about her child?

   b. What is He supposed to do? Does He do it at this time? Compare this verse with Revelation 19:15.

   c. Where does He go?

   d. What happens to the woman after He leaves?

   e. In light of all you observe from the text, who do you think her child is?

   f. What time phrases are associated with the woman? What happens during this period of time? Are there two different times or are they the same thing? Share your reasoning.

∾ Who is the dragon in Revelation 12?

   a. How does the text describe him?
   b. What is his relationship to the woman?
   c. What happens to him? When?
   d. How do people overcome him?
   e. What is the effect on the world when he is cast out of heaven?
   f. How long does he have after he is cast out of heaven?
   g. What does he do to the woman after he is cast out of heaven?

∾ What relationship, if any, do you see between the seventh trumpet in Revelation 11:15-19 and the statement and timing of Revelation 12:10-13?

∾ What is the most significant thing you have learned this week? Why? How is this going to affect you personally?

THOUGHT FOR THE WEEK

The Bible is an absolutely awesome book. Precept by precept, line upon line, God reveals His truth to us. If we will slow down, spend time at His feet, seek the illumination of the Spirit, carefully observe the text and allow Scripture to interpret Scripture, He will lead us and guide us into all truth.

As you have observed Revelation 11 and 12 this week, haven't you been awed by what you saw? Genesis gives us the beginning; Revelation tells us the end. What begins in Genesis, we see completed in Revelation. In Genesis 12 the nation of Israel is called into existence through God's

promise to Abraham. In Revelation 12 the nation of Israel
is still in existence.

In Genesis 3:15 we have the first promise of this Seed,
a Seed born of a woman—a Seed that will destroy the serpent's head. In Revelation we see the defeat of the serpent
and the triumph of Jesus Christ.

The prophecy of the woman and her Seed in Genesis
3:15 was a foreshadowing of Jesus Christ, born from the
tribe of Judah, of the seed of Israel just as Jacob prophesies
in Genesis 49:8-11.

In Genesis 15 God reaffirms His promise of a seed
for a childless Abraham, and he believes God and it is
accounted to him as righteousness. In Galatians 3:16 we read
that "the promises were spoken to Abraham and to his seed.
He does not say, 'And to seeds,' as *referring* to many, but
rather to one, 'And to your seed,' that is, Christ."

And as in Genesis 3:15 there is enmity between the
serpent (who Revelation 12:9 tells us is the dragon, the
devil) and the woman, so that same enmity continues
right through Revelation 12.

The account of the dragon's attempt to devour the
woman's child is simply an account of Herod's attempt to
kill Jesus, born "King of the Jews" (Matthew 2:2) and the
"RULER WHO WILL SHEPHERD . . . ISRAEL" (Matthew 2:6).
Herod, the Roman tetrarch of Galilee, was a pawn of the
serpent of old, the devil, Satan.

Jesus was not only to be King of the Jews, He was to
rule all nations with a rod of iron. But first He had to ful-
fill His role as the Lamb of God. First, He had to die for
the sins of the world, be resurrected from the dead, and
ascend to the Father to prepare a place for us. Then when
all things are ready, the Lamb who is the Lion of Judah

will come and "to him shall be the obedience of the peoples" (Genesis 49:10).

Until then He is seated in heavenly places interceding for us. His day—the day of the Lord—is coming. A time of tribulation—"a great tribulation, such as has not occurred since the beginning of the world until now, nor ever shall" (Matthew 24:21). It will be a time that is prophesied in Daniel 12 and Joel 2. Daniel 7 and 12 tells us that it will last $3\frac{1}{2}$ years. It is a time when the little horn of Daniel 7 will wage war with the saints (the believing Jews) and overpower them for $3\frac{1}{2}$ years until his dominion is "taken away, annihilated and destroyed forever. Then the sovereignty, the dominion, and the greatness of *all* the kingdoms under the whole heaven will be given to the people of the saints of the Highest One; His kingdom *will be* an everlasting kingdom, and all the dominions will serve and obey Him" (Daniel 7:26,27).

Matthew 24 describes this same period of time, telling us of a time of great tribulation, when those in Judea are instructed to flee to the mountains for refuge. How well this seems to parallel the persecution of the woman by the dragon for $3\frac{1}{2}$ years when she is told to flee into the wilderness where she will be protected.

How well this time of outrage by the devil correlates even with what you saw about the multitude before the throne in Revelation 7—a multitude clothed in white robes, a multitude which came out of the great tribulation. Couldn't this be why, after the war in heaven in which the dragon and his angels are kicked out of heaven, it is woe to the earth and to the sea because "the devil has come down to you, having great wrath, knowing that he has only a short time" (Revelation 12:12).

Yet for all the devil's wrath, we can rest confident in the triumph of our God, for with the blowing of the seventh trumpet the mystery of God is finished. No longer do we wonder why God does not move or why He does not take direct action against the devil and his human pawns. At the seventh trumpet "the salvation, and the power, and the kingdom of our God and the authority of His Christ have come" (Revelation 12:10). Satan is kicked out of heaven and the seven bowls are about to be poured out—the bowl judgments which will directly affect the throne of the beast and those who have given allegiance to him. At the seventh trumpet, the temple in heaven is opened and the King is on His way! Hallelujah!

The Mark of the Beast

DAY ONE

Today we are going to learn more about the beast.
Read Revelation 13:1-10. Mark the key words from your
bookmark. Also mark any references to time.

Then, in your notebook start a PROFILE SHEET ON THE
FIRST BEAST. List everything you learn about this beast in
this section and throughout the rest of Revelation.
Examine the text in the light of the 5 W's and an H: How
is this beast described? What does he do? Where does this
beast get his power? How long does he have this power?
What is the extent of his power?

DAY TWO

Read Revelation 13:11-18 and mark the key words
from your bookmark. However, when you see the word
beast in this portion of Scripture, it is a reference to another beast—different from the one mentioned in
Revelation 13:1-10. So mark this beast differently than
you marked the beast of 13:1-10.

In your notebook start another PROFILE SHEET ON
THE SECOND BEAST. List everything you learn about the

second beast from this passage. Once again examine this beast in the light of the 5 W's and an H.

When you finish, go back to Revelation 11:7 to the first mention of the beast. Do you see anything mentioned in conjunction with this beast that might fit in with what you learned in Revelation 13? If so, record it on the appropriate PROFILE SHEET in your notebook and write Revelation 11:7 next to the appropriate beast in the margin of your Bible.

In your notebook make a list of all you learn by marking *those who dwell on the earth, those who dwell in it, (all who dwell on the earth).*[29]

DAY THREE

Read Revelation 13 again and mark every reference to *the image of the beast (an image to the beast*[30]) and to the *mark* of the beast—each in its own distinctive way. In your notebook record all you learn about this mark and about the image of the beast on your PROFILE SHEET ON THE FIRST BEAST.

Also mark the word *worship.* Notice who is worshiped and why.

DAY FOUR

Read Revelation 14. Mark the key words from your bookmark. Also mark the word *angel.* Mark any reference to *Babylon* and add it to your bookmark. Don't forget to mark Babylon's pronouns and synonyms (*great harlot, woman, great city, mother of harlot[s])*[31] and remember to note these on your bookmark. Babylon is about to become a very important word in the text. Also start a PROFILE SHEET ON BABYLON in your notebook and add your insights to it. You will need several pages for this chart.

DAY FIVE

Read Revelation 14 again. Note where you marked the word *angel*. Write in your notebook what happens with each angel mentioned in this chapter. Also record on your PROFILE SHEET ON THE FIRST BEAST any new insights you glean from this chapter on the image of the beast and/or the mark of the beast.

DAY SIX

In Revelation 14:1-5 we see the mention of the 144,000 again. Carefully read the text, asking the 5 W's and an H: What do you learn about these 144,000? How are they described? Where are they? What are they doing? Where did they come from?

Record your observations in your notebook. Then read Revelation 7:1-8 again. Do you think this is the same 144,000? Record your observations in your notebook.

Also add any new insights to your list on God, Jesus, and the Spirit.

Record the events of Revelation 13 and 14 on your EVENTS LIST. Then discern and record the chapter themes of these chapters on the REVELATION AT A GLANCE chart.

DAY SEVEN

 Store in your heart: Revelation 14:9-11 or 14:9,10.
Read and discuss: Revelation 13:1-9,18 and Daniel
7:1-8,16-28. (If you have never studied the book
of Daniel or if the members of your class did not
do The International Inductive Study Series on
Daniel, *God's Blueprint for Prophecy*, drop the references to Daniel out of your reading and discussion time.)

OPTIONAL QUESTIONS FOR DISCUSSION

∾ What did you learn about the first beast of Revelation
13? It would be good to record your insights on a
board if possible so everyone in the class can see them.

a. What is his relationship to the dragon?
b. How is he described?
c. What do you learn about his wound?
d. For how long does he have authority to act? What
   does he do with that authority?
e. Who worships this beast? How? Why?

∾ What did you learn about the second beast of Revelation 13?

a. How is he described?
b. What is his relationship to the first beast?
c. What does he do?
d. How does he relate to those who dwell upon the
   earth?

∾ What did you observe from Revelation 13 and 14 about the image of the beast and the mark of the beast?

   a. What is the image of the beast?

   b. Where does it come from?

   c. What is its purpose?

   d. What happens in relationship to this image?

   e. What is the mark of the beast?

   f. Who receives it? Why?

   g. What are the consequences of not having the mark?

   h. What happens to those who take the mark of the beast? See Revelation 14:9-12.

∾ If you have time, discuss Revelation 14:6-20.

   a. Does everyone on earth have the opportunity to hear the gospel? How? Why? Compare this with Matthew 24:14. (Write this cross-reference in your Bible.)

   b. Do you see a contrast between the worshipers of the beast's image and those mentioned in Revelation 14:12,13? Why do you think this latter group needs to persevere and/or is dying?

   c. How do the angels reap the harvest of the earth? Where is that harvest thrown?

   d. Where is the wine press?

   e. How high does the blood come out from the wine press? For what distance?

Optional—for those who have studied Daniel (*God's Blueprint for Bible Prophecy* in The International Inductive Study Series).

Read Daniel 7:1-8,16-28. Record your insights from the following questions on the board next to your insights on the fourth beast and the little horn of Daniel 7.

a. What do you learn about the fourth beast from this passage?
b. What do you learn about the little or other horn? Where does this horn come from?
c. How long does this horn have power? Over whom? What does he do?
d. What happens to this horn after that period of time?
e. Who rules then?

THOUGHT FOR THE WEEK

Down through the ages men have been fascinated with "the mark of the beast." The fact that the mark is the equivalent of a man's name adding up to 666 has caused much speculation. Yet there is far more given regarding this man than the number of his name. Revelation 13 gives quite a full description of the beast that rules over the whole world for a period of 3½ years. Yet other passages such as Daniel 7 and Daniel 11:36–12:13 throw even more light on him. Daniel 9:26 speaks of the prince who is to come: a man who makes a covenant with many in Israel and then, in the middle of the covenant, puts an end to sacrifice and grain offering; a man who comes on the wing of abominations, who makes desolate or causes horror and yet comes to his decreed destruction. Matthew 24:15 calls him the "ABOMINATION OF DESOLATION" and

2 Thessalonians 2:3 calls him "the man of lawlessness." First John 2:22 and 4:1-6 call him "the antichrist."

When you combine the facts from all these passages, you come up with a composite picture of the beast of Revelation—a life-size portrait of the devil's seed! When the time of his "reign" comes, those who read the Word of God will be able to easily identify him—if anyone has an ear to hear (Revelation 13:9).

Those who hear and believe so as to order their behavior accordingly will receive the reward of the perseverance and faith of the saints. However, those who ignore God's Word and choose to save themselves by taking the mark of the beast can be assured that they will be tormented with fire and brimstone in the presence of the holy angels and in the presence of the Lamb. The smoke of their torment will go up forever and ever and they will have no rest day and night. They will be without excuse, for God will have broadcasted His eternal gospel to every nation, tribe, tongue, and people.

O Beloved, you are studying a sure word of prophecy. If you hear and follow the words of this book, you will be blessed. If you truly heed the Word, won't you find yourself warning people to flee from the wrath which is to come, from the hour of testing that will test all those who dwell on the earth (Revelation 3:10)?

Remember, Jesus is coming and His reward is with Him, to give to everyone according to what he has done (Revelation 22:12). Are you ready?

The Seven Bowls of Wrath

D<small>AY</small> O<small>NE</small>

This week we are going to look at Revelation 15 and 16 and your work load will be lighter. Does that sound good or are you so thrilled at what you are seeing for yourself that it doesn't matter? We pray the latter is true!

Read Revelation 15 and add the words *plague(s)* or *bowl(s)*[32] to your bookmark, marking them in the same way. Mark the key words from your bookmark.

D<small>AY</small> T<small>WO</small>

Read Revelation 15 again. Mark every reference to God. Then add to your notebook list what this chapter teaches about God and about His wrath. Also note who is singing the song of Moses, what the song is about, how it is directed, and the context in which it is being sung. Record your insights in your notebook.

D<small>AY</small> T<small>HREE</small>

Read Revelation 16. Mark the key words from your

bookmark. Also mark *repent* as you have marked it
before. There's been no actual reference to His second
coming or actual coming to earth since Revelation 3, but
you'll see some now!

After you mark *Babylon,* add what you learn to your
PROFILE SHEET ON BABYLON in your notebook.

DAY FOUR

Read Revelation 16 again. Record everything you
learn about the beast from this chapter on your PROFILE
SHEET ON THE FIRST BEAST in your notebook. Record
anything you observe about the false prophet (the second
beast) on your PROFILE SHEET ON THE SECOND BEAST.
Note the company of the false prophet.

Now fill in the section on the bowls on the chart THE
SEVEN SEALS, TRUMPETS, AND BOWLS (page 140).

DAY FIVE

Read Revelation 15 and 16 again. Then record the
events of these chapters on your EVENTS LIST.

Add insights to your list on God and Jesus.

Identify and record the themes of Revelation 15 and
16 on the REVELATION AT A GLANCE chart.

DAY SIX

Now that you have completed your chart THE SEVEN
SEALS, TRUMPETS, AND BOWLS, you need to take a good

look at the chart and the information you have collected. As you look at this chart, ask yourself the following questions. (You may want to write these questions and your answers in your notebook.)

1. Are the seals, trumpets, and bowls different or are they the same?
2. How do the seals, trumpets, and bowls compare to one another in severity?
3. What happens at the end of the seventh seal? the seventh trumpet? the seventh bowl?
4. How do the seals, trumpets, and bowls relate to one another in their occurrence? Do they occur at the same time or do they follow each other? If you have any question about this, go back and look at Revelation 11:14,15.

DAY SEVEN

Store in your heart: Revelation 16:15.
Read and discuss: Revelation 16:1-21.

OPTIONAL QUESTIONS FOR DISCUSSION

∽ What did you learn about the bowl judgments from Revelation 15 and 16?

a. What is their relationship to the wrath of God?
b. Can you name or list what happens with the pouring out of each bowl?

    c. As you look at the bowl judgments, observe the direct references to the beast. What do you learn about the bowls and their relationship to the beast and/or his followers?

∾ What happens to Babylon in the bowl judgments?

    a. How does the judgment of the seventh bowl compare with Revelation 14:8?

    b. What does this tell you about Revelation 14:8 and its timing? Does it appear that the purpose of Revelation 14 is to give an overview of what is about to occur?

∾ When you looked at the chart THE SEVEN SEALS, TRUMPETS, AND BOWLS, what did you learn about the relationship between the seals, the trumpets, and the bowls?

    a. Are the seals, trumpets, and bowls different, or are they the same?

    b. How do the seals, trumpets, and bowls compare to one another in severity?

    c. What happens at the end of the seventh seal? the seventh trumpet? the seventh bowl?

    d. How do the seals, trumpets, and bowls relate to one another in their occurrence? Do they occur at the same time, or does one follow another? Look at Revelation 11:14,15. What indicates that the trumpets follow one another in order? (Look at the time phrases you marked when you studied Revelation 11, i.e., *past, coming quickly*.)

    e. Do you think the seventh seal brings forth the seven trumpets, and then the seventh trumpet brings forth the seven bowls?

∾ What happens at the sixth bowl?

    a. What role do the beast, the dragon, and the false prophet play in this bowl?

    b. What is the relationship of these three to one another? Look at what you have recorded up to this point on your notebook PROFILE SHEETS on these characters.

    c. Discuss who is gathered, where they are gathered, how they come to this place, and the purpose of their gathering.

∾ What do you think is the purpose of Revelation 16:15, which is in parentheses in the middle of the sixth bowl?

    a. Who is speaking?

    b. To whom? Remember to whom Revelation was written. Look at Revelation 1:11.

    c. What is the message?

    d. What have you seen about garments and the references to them up to this point? (See also Revelation 3:4,5,18.)

THOUGHT FOR THE WEEK

Once the Lamb of God takes the seven-sealed book from the hand of God and breaks it open, the process of redeeming the earth from the prince of this world is set in motion. One seal will be broken, then a second, third, fourth, and fifth seal. With the breaking of the sixth seal, people will get the picture. They will recognize that God is behind it all and cry for deliverance from the wrath which is to come.

But they won't have seen anything yet. With the breaking of the seventh seal, there will be the blasts of the seven trumpets with the last three bringing increasing woes upon the earth.

Finally, when the seventh trumpet is blown, God will move in a direct assault against those who have refused to repent. His wrath will be poured out in seven bowls of judgment. Those who choose to follow the beast, to receive his mark, will find themselves in the path of God's judgment. They had the opportunity to hear the eternal gospel, for God declared it to every nation, tribe, tongue, and people, but they did not listen.

Thus the line is drawn; the sides are clearly identified. The wrath of God will be poured out upon them. But when the fifth bowl is poured out, rather than repent, they blasphemed the God of heaven because of their pain and their sores. Life knocked at their door but they chose to dwell in death.

The kings of the earth will gather together at Har-Magedon (Armageddon) to make war against God Almighty—not understanding, not believing that some-day every knee will bow and every tongue will confess that Jesus Christ is Lord to the glory of God the Father.

With the pouring out of the seventh bowl the wrath of God is finished. Just as was said at the sounding of the seventh trumpet which introduced the seven bowls, God Almighty has taken His great power and has begun to reign.

In those seven bowls, God's wrath comes in full force. Like an avalanche, no one can stop it. While the first bowl will be a direct attack against those who take the mark of the beast; the fifth bowl will be poured out on the kingdom of the beast.

No wonder those who had been victorious over the beast—those who did not take the mark of the beast, who did not love their lives unto death but overcame him by the blood of the Lamb and the word of their testimony—will sing their song of victory:

> Great and marvelous are Thy works, O Lord God, the Almighty; righteous and true are Thy ways, Thou King of the nations. Who will not fear, O Lord, and glorify Thy name? For Thou alone art holy; for ALL THE NATIONS WILL COME AND WORSHIP BEFORE THEE, for Thy righteous acts have been revealed (Revelation 15:3,4).

These are the people who, during this time, believe that Jesus is the Christ, the Son of God and, even in the face of persecution and death, keep the commandments of God and hold to the testimony of Jesus Christ.

And what about you, Beloved? The book of Revelation was written for the church so that she would know the things which will shortly come to pass. God promised Jesus would come—and when things are put in motion, it will happen quickly. Like an avalanche, once it starts nothing or no one can stop it. It overcomes everything in its path.

O Beloved, have you heard His Word? He is coming quickly. You are "sons of light," of the day; therefore you are not to sleep as others, but to be alert and sober. God calls you to persevere. Keep your garments white; don't soil them, for the time is coming when you will walk in white, hand-in-hand with the Lord. Do not fear those who can kill the body; rather fear Him who is able to cast both body and soul into hell.

Continue in the faith, for this is the victory that over-comes the world. And who is the one who overcomes the world? It is the one who believes that Jesus is the Christ, the Son of God. Jesus will not erase your name from the book of life if you are truly His child. He will confess your name before His Father and the angels.

Those who save their lives will lose them, but those who lose their lives for Him and for the sake of the gospel will save them.

There are some defeats that are more victorious than victories!

Solving the Mystery
of Babylon

Day One

Read Revelation 17 and mark the key words from your bookmark. Note what Revelation 17:7 promises to tell you. Also mark the words *kings* (and its pronouns) and *kingdom*[33] and add these to your bookmark.

Now, make a list in your notebook of everything you learn about the kings from this chapter. Then on your PROFILE SHEET ON THE FIRST BEAST add your insights about the beast. As you record what you've seen about the beast in this chapter, be certain you haven't missed any pertinent information by asking the 5 W's and an H such as:

1. How is the beast described?
2. What do the earth dwellers wonder about in respect to the beast?
3. How are these earth dwellers described?
4. What is the relationship of the beast to the seven heads?
5. What are the seven heads?
6. What are the seven mountains?
7. What is the beast's relationship to the ten horns?
8. What are the ten horns?

9. How do the beast and the ten horns relate to
the Lamb?
10. What does the Lamb do to them?

Read Revelation 17:9,10 very carefully, letting Scripture speak for itself. Don't read anything into the text that is not there. Revelation 17:10 tells you what the seven heads, and the seven mountains are. Record any insights in your notebook.

DAY TWO

Read Revelation 17 again. When you finish reading through the chapter, determine how you are going to mark the references to the *woman*. Did you decide to mark this word the same way you marked Babylon? Why or why not? Then mark every reference to the *woman*, including any synonyms or pronouns that refer to her.

DAY THREE

List everything you see about the woman from observing Revelation 17 on your PROFILE ON BABYLON. Again ask questions in order to be sure you've accurately observed the text!

1. Who is this woman?
2. How is she described? (What adjectives are used to describe her? How is she dressed?)

3. Where does she sit?
4. What is the relationship of this woman to the saints and the witnesses of Jesus?
5. What is this woman? What is her name?
6. What will happen to her?
7. How will it happen?
8. Why will it happen?

DAY FOUR

Read Revelation 18. Today don't mark any key words from your bookmark. Only mark references to *Babylon* and any reference to *one day* and *one hour*.

DAY FIVE

Read Revelation 18 again and mark the key words from your bookmark. You'll see two references to *fine linen* but you won't want to mark those as you have earlier references to *white garments* or *white robe(s)*. Why? Note the contrast between these references in this chapter and the references just noted that you marked earlier.

List everything you learn about Babylon from Revelation 18 in your notebook on your PROFILE SHEET ON BABYLON.

Then, observing every place where you marked *one day* and *one hour*, note what happens in that one day and

in that one hour. Record your insights in your notebook.

DAY SIX

Record what you learn from Revelation 17 and 18 on
your EVENTS LIST. Also record the themes for these on your
REVELATION AT A GLANCE chart. Then record any new
insights on Jesus, God, and the Spirit on your notebook list.

When you finish, review what you've noted on your
EVENTS LIST and your PROFILE SHEET ON BABYLON. Just
from observing the Scriptures, what have you learned
about Babylon? How does it compare with what you have
been taught about Babylon? Think about how important
it is to study God's Word yourself so you know firsthand
what God's Word says. This personal study approach
counteracts the common repeat-by-rote approach which
can propagate error—especially in these days of radio and
television.

We are proud of you, friend, for disciplining yourself
to study the Word on your own. Persevere!

DAY SEVEN

Store in your heart: Revelation 17:7,18.
Read and discuss: Revelation 17:3–18:24.

OPTIONAL QUESTIONS FOR DISCUSSION

∾ What is going to be explained to you in Revelation
17:7?

ぺ Who is the woman of Revelation 17:7?

    a. How do you know?

    b. What is the woman? (Remember to cite verse references.)

    c. Does the description of the woman change from Revelation 17 to Revelation 18?

ぺ What do you learn from Revelation 18:10?

ぺ What does the woman get drunk on?

ぺ What is the relationship of the woman to the beast?

ぺ What do you learn about the beast? What is the mystery of the beast?

    a. How is the beast described in Revelation 17? What do you learn about him from this chapter?

    b. Is the beast ever a king?

    c. What is the relationship of the beast to the seven kings?

ぺ What do you learn about the ten horns from Revelation 17?

    a. What is the relationship of the beast to these horns?

    b. What is the response of the ten horns to the Lamb?

    c. Who do you think the Lamb is? Why? (Compare Revelation 17:14 with Revelation 5.)

    d. How do the ten horns feel about the woman?

    e. How does what they do to her compare with what Revelation 18 tells us happens to her?

    f. Why do the horns do this to the woman?

    g. Who is behind what happens to the woman?

ぺ From Revelation 18, what do you learn about the destruction of Babylon?

a. What is Babylon called throughout this chapter?
b. How does this compare with Revelation 17:18? What is she called there?
c. Using the Scripture text only, do you think Revelation 17 and 18 describe one Babylon or two Babylons? Give your reasons.
d. How swift is Babylon's destruction?
e. How does Revelation 18:2 compare with Revelation 14:8 and 16:19? What do these verses tell you about the timing of the destruction of Babylon?
f. What is the response of various groups of people to Babylon's destruction?

∾ What is God's word in Revelation 18 to His people in respect to Babylon?

a. Who do you think He is calling His people in Revelation 18:4?
b. What does this tell you about some of the people living at the time of the seventh bowl?

∾ What have you learned this week that has really impacted your life?

THOUGHT FOR THE WEEK

For many years a common teaching has been that the harlot, Babylon the Great of Revelation 17, is the Roman Catholic Church—"mystery Babylon, mother of harlots." We have been told that the seven mountains (hills) she sits on are the seven hills of Rome. We have been taught that Revelation 17 presents the "Ecclesiastical Babylon" while Revelation 18 represents the "political Babylon." Is this what you observed in the text? What do the Scriptures—not the commentaries—say?

First, Revelation 17 tells us that the woman is the great city that reigns over the kings of the earth. The name on her forehead is "BABYLON THE GREAT, THE MOTHER OF HARLOTS AND OF THE ABOMINATIONS OF THE EARTH."

Throughout Revelation 18, Babylon is also referred to as a city. Where is this city? Are the seven mountains on which the woman sits the seven mountains or hills of the city of Rome?

Revelation 17:9,10 tells us that the seven mountains are seven kings and that the beast himself is an eighth king—but one of the seven, and the beast himself is going to destruction.

The beast is described as the one who was, and is not, and is about to come up out of the abyss and go to destruction. The beast that puts to death the two witnesses in Revelation 11 is described as the one who comes up out of the abyss. How does all this compare to Revelation 13:3 when we read that one of the heads was slain and his fatal wound was healed?

Let's reason together. Could it be that the beast described here, as part of the seven kings was killed, then sometime before the death of the two witnesses he was "resurrected"—coming up out of the abyss? Could it be that at this same time, Satan is cast down to earth? Thus, Satan—the dragon—gives his power to the beast and it kills the two witnesses. When he kills the two witnesses who no one else can stop or kill, the world sits up and takes notice. The beast who was one of the seven and died, now is also an eighth king and the whole world follows him. And the persecution begins!

First the persecution is directed toward the Jews. The beast moves into the "Beautiful Land," Israel, walks into their temple, stands in the Holy of Holies, and declares himself God. He is the abomination of desolation spoken of by Daniel and Matthew and is the man of lawlessness of 2 Thessalonians 2.

So the woman flees into the wilderness. Those in Judea do not even get their coats; they flee to where God has prepared a place for the woman, Israel, for $3\frac{1}{2}$ years.

It might be at this time that the second beast (the false prophet) makes an image of the first beast and causes people to take his mark and, thus, worship the image of the beast. Those who refuse to take his mark will not be able to buy or sell and will suffer great persecution. The beast, along with the ten horns (kings), sets up their headquarters in Babylon. (Could this be in the literal Babylon [Iran]? All that was prophesied in the Old Testament has not yet come to pass in respect to the literal city of Babylon.)

Babylon is a city that will persecute those who keep their garments unsoiled, who love not their lives unto death. It is a city in which the blood of prophets and of saints and of all who have been slain on the earth is found. This city has been in opposition to God and His rule in their lives since the days of Nimrod, as recorded in Genesis (see chapter 10). This is the city of those who conquered Judah and destroyed Jerusalem in 586 B.C. This is the city that is being rebuilt in Iran . . . and exists even today. Could it possibly be the city of Revelation 17 and 18? Time will tell.

The beast's headquarters will be in Babylon, but the beast's relationship with the woman is not all that it appears to be. The beast and the 10 kings who have no kingdom, but who give their authority to the beast, want to see her destroyed. Thus, God uses them to execute His will and judgment upon Babylon the Great.

In one hour—in one day—at the pouring out of the seventh bowl, Babylon is destroyed forever as she receives the cup of the wine of the fierce wrath of God. When the seventh trumpet is blown, God begins to reign in order to show who He is.

At the pouring out of the sixth bowl the armies of the world, some coming across the dry river bed of the Euphrates, will gather at Har-Magedon to make war against God and His people.

When God pours out the seventh and final bowl of wrath, the armies of the earth will see from a great distance the smoke of the burning Babylon, the great city of wealth. And the beast and the ten kings will go forth to wage war against the Lamb, but the Lamb will overcome them because He is Lord of lords and King of kings.

Look up! The King is coming and those who are coming with Him are the called and chosen and faithful. That's you! That's us, my friend! Persevere for He is coming and His reward is with Him.

Exactly What Happens When Jesus Comes?

DAY ONE

Read Revelation 19 and mark your key words. Be careful that you don't miss any. We are coming to the conclusion of Revelation and marking these key words will help you get a complete picture of the subjects you've been studying, such as Babylon, the beast, and the nations. Mark and add the word *bride*[34] to your bookmark.

DAY TWO

Today we are going to look at Revelation 19 paragraph by paragraph. As you look at each paragraph, write down the theme of the paragraph in order to gain a good analysis of this important and exciting chapter. Record the themes in your notebook by paragraph:

Revelation 19:1-6a
Revelation 19:6b-10
Revelation 19:11-16
Revelation 19:17,18
Revelation 19:19-21

This gives you the information you need to fill out your EVENTS LIST so record your insights for Revelation 19.

DAY THREE

Read through Revelation 19 a third time. This time mark every reference to "the One who sat upon the white horse, who is called Faithful and True" (19:11). Don't forget to mark any synonyms and/or pronouns that refer to this person. When you finish your observations, list in your notebook all you observe from marking these references. Then think about what you have seen. (It's interesting to compare what you read here with what you recorded about the description of Jesus on your chart JESUS' MESSAGES TO THE CHURCHES (pages 47-51) and with the description of Jesus in Revelation 1.)

Add your insights about Jesus to the list in your notebook.

Compare the description of those who come on white horses with "The Word of God" in Revelation 19:14 with Revelation 19:7,8. Are they the same group of people?

Before you decide, also look at Revelation 17:14. What do you think? Why? Record your insights in your notebook.

DAY FOUR

Add to your PROFILE SHEETS what you learn from this chapter about Babylon, the beast, and the false prophet (the second beast of Revelation 13). Also add insights on God and Jesus to your list and record any new information you see on the second coming of Christ.

After you finish your insights on Babylon, you might want to look up Jeremiah 51:24-26, which speaks of the final destruction of Babylon. You may want to mark this as a cross-reference by writing it in your Bible next to Revelation 19:1-6 (which deals with the destruction of Babylon).

DAY FIVE

When you marked your key words, you marked the phrases *wages war* and *makes war*.[35] Look at where war occurs in this chapter and record in your notebook what you learn about it. Now read Revelation 16:13-16 and 17:14. In your notebook, record the details of the war mentioned in these passages and then compare them with what you observed in Revelation 19. Think about it. Do all these refer to the same war? Record your insights in your notebook.

Now look at Revelation 14:17-20 and compare it with Revelation 19:15. What do you see? Record your insights in your notebook.

DAY SIX

Today we are going to have a little fun by looking up some Old Testament references about the coming of the Messiah (the Christ). Look at these Scriptures in light of all you have observed this week. If you think these verses give added insight on the coming of the Lord in Revelation 19, then note them as cross-references in your Bible.

As you read these references, be certain to keep the 5 W's and an H in mind.

First, look up Isaiah 34:5-8. Watch what this passage of Scripture says about the sword, blood, and Edom. Compare the blood here with Revelation 14:20 and 19:13; then find the locations on the map on page 117.

Read Isaiah 63:1-6 and watch where this person comes from, why His garments are stained, and what has stained them. Also look at Revelation 19:15.

Compare Isaiah 11:1-5 to Revelation 19:15.

Read and compare Psalm 2:1-9, then Revelation 2:26,27; 5:10 with 19:15.

DAY SEVEN

Store in your heart: Revelation 19:15,16.
Read and Discuss: Revelation 19.

OPTIONAL QUESTIONS FOR DISCUSSION

∾ What is Revelation 19 about?

a. Review the themes of this chapter paragraph by paragraph.

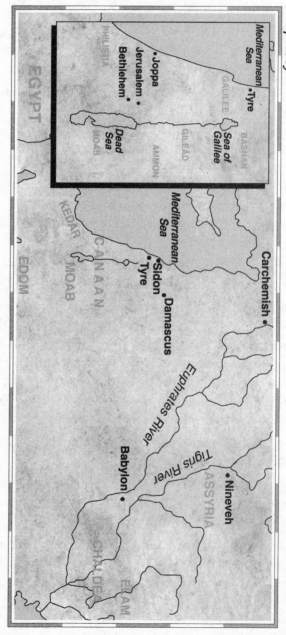

The Nations of Jeremiah's Prophecy

b. Discuss what you learn about the place, persons, or events in each paragraph.

❧ What did you learn from Revelation 19 about the coming of the Lord?

a. How is the Word of God described in this chapter?
b. From where and to where does He come?
c. What happens when He comes?
d. What happens to the nations?
e. What happens to the kings?
f. What happens to the beast and the false prophet?
g. Who comes with Him?
h. How are they described? What other Scriptures give insights on this?

❧ What did you learn from looking up the cross-references on Day 6? Discuss them one by one.

a. What questions do they pose?
b. How are you going to find the answers to these questions? Remember this is a survey course on Revelation. Questions are good because they cause you to dig in the Word of God. (Note we said "the Word," not commentaries, for you'll find all sorts of opinions on Revelation—some good, some weird.)

❧ What is the most significant thing you saw or learned in this week's study?

❧ How has all that you are learning impacted or affected your thoughts about God? Your relationship with Him? Your life in general?

❧ Revelation 1:3 promises a blessing to those who read, hear, and follow the words of Revelation. What have you read and heard that you need to heed and do?

THOUGHT FOR THE WEEK

What is the sequence of events surrounding the coming of the King of kings? After two years of writing and doing our four Precept Upon Precept Inductive study courses, I (Kay) want to share with you how I see things transpiring. This will give you something to think about and examine. As I explain what I believe might happen, you can follow along on the map on page 117.

First, with the pouring out of the sixth bowl, the kings of the whole world are summoned by unclean spirits to the battlefield of battlefields, the plain of Megiddo, for the war of the great day of God, the Almighty.

Then, *second,* the seventh bowl is poured out and Babylon, that great city which rules over the kings of the earth, will be destroyed by fire. The city that the beast carried is destroyed, yet the beast lives. His heart is still intent on war against the people of God—God's chosen and elect nation of Israel. Although many people who lived in Judea fled into the wilderness of Edom when the abomination of desolation stood in the holy place declaring himself to be God, still Jerusalem remained.

Third, I believe the beast, leading the armies of the earth, will proceed through the valley of Jehoshaphat to ravage Jerusalem just as Zechariah 14:2,3 tells us: "I will gather all the nations against Jerusalem to battle, and the city will be captured, the houses plundered, the women ravished, and half of the city exiled, but the rest of the people will not be cut off from the city. Then the LORD will go forth and fight against those nations, as when He fights on a day of battle."

This leads us to the *fourth* event. Revelation tells us that when the Lord comes He is clothed with a robe dipped in blood and that He treads the wine press of the fierce wrath of God. Isaiah describes Him as one who comes from Edom, with garments of glowing colors from Bozrah. Then he records the following: "Why is Your apparel red, and Your garments like the one who treads in the wine press?"

To which he replies, "I have trodden the wine trough alone, and from the peoples there was no man with Me. I also trod them in My anger, and trampled them in My wrath; and their lifeblood is sprinkled on My garments, and I stained all My raiment. For the day of vengeance was in My heart, and My year of redemption has come . . . and I trod down the peoples in My anger, and made them drunk in My wrath, and I poured out their lifeblood on the earth" (Isaiah 63:2-4,6).

As we piece all these Scriptures together, it seems that the scenario of events surrounding the coming of the Lord might occur something like this: Following the attack on Jerusalem by the nations, it could be that the armies, led by the beast, might set out toward Edom to destroy those Jews who fled into the wilderness approximately $3\frac{1}{2}$ years earlier. Then the Lord will come first to Edom for His elect people whom He nourished in the wilderness for the past $3\frac{1}{2}$ years. "For My sword is satiated in heaven, behold it shall descend for judgment upon Edom. . . . For the LORD has a sacrifice in Bozrah, and a great slaughter in the land of Edom. . . . For the LORD has a day of vengeance, a year of recompense for the cause of Zion" (Isaiah 34:5,6,8).

Next the Lord would come from Edom up the valley of Jehoshaphat. As He comes, He meets the opposing armies and tramples out the wine press of the fierce wrath of God, destroying them with the sword that comes out of his mouth, leaving the valley flowing with blood at the depth of the bridles on the horses. "Hasten and come, all you surrounding nations, and gather yourselves there. Bring down, O LORD, Thy mighty ones. Let the nations be aroused and come up to the valley of Jehoshaphat, for there I will sit to judge all the surrounding nations. Put in the sickle, for the harvest is ripe. Come, tread, for the wine press is full; the vats overflow, for their wickedness is great" (Joel 3:11-13).

Fifth, "in that day His feet will stand on the Mount of Olives, which is in front of Jerusalem on the east; and the Mount of Olives will be split in its middle from east to west by a very large valley, so that half of the mountain will move toward the north and the other half toward the south. . . . Then the LORD, my God, will come, and all the holy ones with Him! . . . And the LORD will be king over all the earth; in that day the LORD will be the only one, and His name the only one. . . . Then it will come about that any who are left of all the nations that went against Jerusalem will go up from year to year to worship the King, the LORD of hosts, and to celebrate the Feast of Booths" (Zechariah 14:4,5,9,16).

Even so, come quickly Lord Jesus. . . .

WEEK TWELVE

The Reign of Christ and the Lake of Fire

DAY ONE

Read Revelation 20. At this point don't worry about marking key words or time phrases. Read now to simply get the overall picture of the events in this chapter.

Now read Revelation 20 again. Mark every reference to the *lake of fire*[36] and add it to your bookmark. Go back to Revelation 19:20 and mark the phrase there too. Also mark the other key words from your bookmark. Mark all references to time.

DAY TWO

Read Revelation 20 again. This time mark the phrase *the dead* and the word *death,* but mark them in such a way as to distinguish one from the other. When you finish, list in your notebook everything you learn from marking these words.

Record on your PROFILE SHEETS anything you learn from Revelation 20 about the beast or the false prophet. Add to your list on the dragon you began in Week 7 anything more you see about him. Make sure you marked all the synonyms for the dragon so you get a complete profile of him from these verses.

DAY THREE

Read through Revelation 20 again. As you read this time, watch for the various events that are covered in this chapter. Mark every reference to *the first resurrection* and *the second death,* each in its own distinctive way. Put the phrase *the second death* on your bookmark.

DAY FOUR

As you saw yesterday, Revelation 20 covers a series of events. Spend today carefully observing the events of Revelation 20:1-10. Record your insights on Revelation 20:1-10 on your EVENTS LIST. As you review what you saw yesterday, remember to ask questions using the 5 W's and an H:

Who are the characters involved in each event?
What happens in this event?
When does it happen? For how long?
Where does it happen?
Why does it occur?
How does it come to pass?
What is the end result of each event?

DAY FIVE

There's one last event covered in Revelation 20:11-15 that you will want to observe closely. Read this passage again and mark the phrase *according to their deeds.*[37] Then examine these verses in the light of the 5 W's and an H.

Record your insights on your EVENTS LIST for the chapter.

After you finish, go back and observe what this chapter teaches about the second death. Note who is and who is not affected by the second death.

DAY SIX

Today we'll take a closer look at the great white throne judgment and some cross-references that might shed light on the way these people are judged. Read Revelation 20:11-15 again. Note who is at this judgment and who is not because this is very important.

Deeds is an important word in the book of Revelation. Review what you learned from marking the phrase *according to their deeds*[38] in Revelation 20:11-15. Then go back to Revelation 2 and 3 and look at every place you marked the word *deeds*[39] and make a list of what you learn.

Are we saved by our deeds, our works, or are they simply a manifestation of what has or hasn't taken place in our hearts and lives in relationship to Jesus Christ and the salvation from sin which He offers us if we believe in Him? Look up the following verses, note them in your notebook under Revelation 20, and then record what you learn from each passage: Ephesians 2:8-10; Titus 3:5-8; and Romans 2:4-11. (As you look at these verses watch for the words *deeds* or *works*. Note whether the person is doing good or doing evil and the consequences of each.)

Look up the following verses and note what you learn about "the day of judgment" in respect to possible degrees of judgment in relation to the light and opportunity a person has: Matthew 10:14,15; 11:21-24; 12:41,42; Mark 12:38-40; 2 Corinthians 11:13-15. Now go back and compare what you've seen with what you learned about the great white throne judgment. Remember who is at this judgment and who isn't. Note the basis of their judgment. Think about the justness of God even when judging those who are not saved.

Record the theme of Revelation 20 on your REVELATION AT A GLANCE chart and add new insights to your list on God and Jesus.

DAY SEVEN

Store in your heart: Revelation 20:6.
Read and discuss: Revelation 20:4-6,11-15.

OPTIONAL QUESTIONS FOR DISCUSSION

∾ What are the main events covered in Revelation 20?

    a. List them on the board in the order in which they are described in Revelation 20.

    b. Note who participates in each event, where it occurs, when it occurs, how long it lasts, and the results or consequences of each event.

    c. Do you think the events of Revelation 20 are laid out in the order of their occurrence? How can you tell?

∾ In light of all you have seen in the book of Revelation, do the references to the $3^1/_2$ years seem literal or figurative? What about the 1000 years mentioned six times in the first seven verses of Revelation 20? Are they literal or figurative? Give the reason for your answer.

∾ What did you learn from your study of the judgment of those who are present at the great white throne?

∾ If all the people in verse 11 are going to be thrown into the lake of fire, why are they being judged according to their deeds?

    a. Will they all suffer the same punishment?

    b. Discuss what you learned this week when you looked up: Ephesians 2:8-10; Titus 3:5-8; Romans 2:4-11; Matthew 10:14,15; 11:21-24; 12:41,42; Mark 12:38-40; 2 Corinthians 11:13-15.

∾ If there is time, discuss the fate of the beast, of the false prophet, and of Satan, the dragon. Note where they go and when.

    a. Why is Satan bound for 1000 years?

    b. What does he do when he is released?

    c. Where does he go when he is released?

    d. What happens to him?

∾ What have you learned from your study this week that you hadn't known before? How is all this going to affect the way you live?

THOUGHT FOR THE WEEK

Down through the annals of time, the hope of both the Jews and the church of Jesus Christ has been the coming of the Messiah to reign as King of kings and Lord of lords. When that day dawns, hope will become substance.

Then the nations of the earth will see that every word of God is true and those who have clung to Him in faith will be vindicated. On that great and glorious day, those who seemed wise in the wisdom of the world will be deemed foolish, and the foolish in the eyes of the world will be seen as wise.

Satan's true nature as the father of lies will be laid bare. Those who survived the holocaust of the great tribulation will see the Son of Man coming "from heaven with His mighty angels in flaming fire to give relief to you who are afflicted," but "dealing out retribution to those who do not know God and to those who do not obey the gospel of our Lord Jesus. And these will pay the penalty of eternal destruction," in the lake of fire "away from the presence of the Lord and from the glory of His power" (2 Thessalonians 1:7-9).

And "when the Son of Man comes in His glory, and all the angels with Him, then He will sit on His glorious throne. And all the nations will be gathered before Him . . ." (Matthew 25:31,32). They will be the multitudes who physically survived the judgments of the seals, trumpets, and bowls. There will be multitudes in the valley of decision as He separates the sheep from the goats on the basis of the way these individuals, in their respective nations, treated His holy and chosen people, the Jews.

Those who do not consider them—who do not feed them or give them something to quench their thirst, or invite them in or care for them when they are sick, or visit them when in prison—will be immediately condemned to eternal punishment. But those people who do the opposite—caring for and loving God's elect people the

Jews—will enter into eternal life, their deeds reflecting the conviction of their hearts.

At this time there will be a great resurrection—the first resurrection, the resurrection unto life. Those who were beheaded because of the testimony of Jesus and because of the Word of God and those who refused to save their lives by taking the mark of the beast will be given a resurrection unto eternal life. And they will rule and reign on this earth with the Lord Jesus Christ for 1000 years.

It seems from Isaiah 65:19-25 that during that time those who are living when Jesus returns will give birth to children—children who will have to decide whether or not they are going to give their allegiance to the King of kings, children who will have to decide if they are going to believe on Him and submit their lives to Him. Those who don't will die before they reach the age of 100. At that time there will be 1000 years of peace on earth. The wolf and the lamb will graze together and the lion will eat straw like an ox. The enemy, the former prince of this world, will be bound so that he cannot deceive the nations he once ruled.

Jesus Christ will govern the earth until all have been brought under His footstool. Those who overcome will rule and reign with Him as well as David and the 12 apostles. However, at the end of the thousand years Satan will be loosed from his bottomless pit and will go out for one last time to deceive the nations. And some will be deceived and in their deception they will think they can conquer our Lord's earthly Jerusalem, and the Jews who have become the praise of all the earth. Yet fire will come down out of heaven and devour him and all those whom he deceived in that short time.

It will be enough. Jesus' enemies will be made His footstool! "The heavens will pass away with a roar and the elements will be destroyed with intense heat, and the earth and its works will be burned up. . . . [There will be] new heavens and a new earth, in which righteousness dwells" (2 Peter 3:10,13). It will be the day of God!

Then all the dead, great and small, from the time of Adam and Eve and the creation of this present heavens and earth, through the time of their destruction—they who have never passed from death to life because they did not put their faith in the first coming of the Messiah, the Christ—will stand at the great white throne of God. There they will be condemned to eternal punishment in the lake of fire which is the second death, where the worm dies not and the fire is not quenched. They are twice dead because they refused to believe on the One who is "the way, and the truth, and the life" (John 14:6), the only One through whom mankind can come to God. They will spend eternity with an unholy trinity—the beast, the false prophet, and the devil himself. They will be without excuse (Romans 1:18-20). Their punishment will be eternal, but the degree of depth of that punishment will depend on how they lived while on the earth. The severity of the lake of fire will be according to their deeds. They will be judged in accordance with the truth they had and the way they responded to it. God is a just God. The wicked who have been more rebellious, more evil than others, who have had more light, more opportunity, and yet refused the Messiah will be punished accordingly.

And what about those who obtained righteousness by faith, a righteousness as Adam and Eve, Abraham and

Sarah, and other Old Testament saints obtained by looking forward in faith? And what about those who were declared righteous by looking at or back to Jesus' life, death, and resurrection? These people, who looked forward in faith to the coming of Messiah and those who looked back in faith at His first coming, will not stand for judgment at the great white throne. Their names are still in the book of life and are recorded in the Lamb's book of life. We will look at the destiny of the righteous in our final lesson on Revelation next week.

Just remember, Beloved, that while my understanding of these prophetic passages might not be perfect—or may not agree with yours—it does not negate the fact that Jesus is coming and His reward is with Him (Revelation 22:6-12). He will rule as King of kings, Lord of lords! So bow before Him now. Let Him have full reign of your life today. It is the one decision you will wish you had made sooner!

What Is
Heaven Like?

DAY ONE

Read Revelation 21 and mark any key words you find from your list. Also mark in a distinctive way every reference to the *new Jerusalem*[40] *(the city,*[41] *the holy city)*. Be sure to mark pronouns which refer to the city.

Note what this chapter is all about—what John is seeing.

DAY TWO

Read Revelation 21 again. Make sure you marked *nations, the second death, the lake,*[42] and *bride*.

When you finish your observations, record in your notebook what you see from this chapter about the lake of fire (which is the second death), the nations, and the bride.

DAY THREE

Read through Revelation 21 again. This time make sure you have marked every reference to God. Then add what you learn about Him from Revelation 21 to the list in your notebook.

DAY FOUR

Today, make a list in your notebook of everything you see in Revelation 21 about the new Jerusalem, the tabernacle of God. Leave space for the insights you'll gain tomorrow. Be sure to examine what you have observed about the new Jerusalem in light of the 5 W's and an H. As you look at the new Jerusalem, notice what you learn about this city in respect to "the temple."

Note who is going to live in the new Jerusalem—and if it's you, get excited! If it's not—repent and believe!

DAY FIVE

Read Revelation 22—your final chapter of study! Mark any key words from your bookmark. Also mark the phrases *heed(s) the words*,[43] *this book, the tree of life*,[44] *the city (the holy city)*.

Record in your notebook, on the list you began yesterday, any new information about the new Jerusalem. Also list what you learn from this chapter about the tree of life.

When you finish, observe and list what you learn from Revelation 21 and 22 about the nations. Are they different from "the bride"? How?

DAY SIX

Read through Revelation 22 again today. Carefully observe what John is doing in this final chapter. Note what is covered at the beginning of the chapter and then what follows.

List everything you learn from marking *this book*. Also list everything you learn from marking the references to the Lord's coming throughout Revelation.

Notice the different groups John refers to in this final exhortation. Go back and read Revelation 1 again and compare what is being said at the beginning of the book with what is said at the end.

Add new insights to your list on Jesus and the Spirit. Also add any new insights on God for this last chapter.

On your EVENTS LIST, briefly record the event(s) covered in Revelation 21 and 22. Also record the themes of these chapters on the REVELATION AT A GLANCE chart.

DAY SEVEN

Store in your heart: Revelation 21:4,5 and/or 22:7 or 12.
Read and discuss: Revelation 21:1-10,22; 22:5,16-21.

OPTIONAL QUESTIONS FOR DISCUSSION

~ What is the main theme(s) of Revelation 21 and 22?

~ Chronologically, when do the events of chapters 21 and 22 occur in relationship to the other events in Revelation?

a. When John was told to write the book of Revelation, what was he to write? (Make sure the class refers to Revelation 1:19.)

b. Draw a time line. Put a cross at the beginning of the time line:

† _____

c. Ask the class where on the time line they would put the following events:

1) the first three chapters of Revelation
2) Revelation 4 and 5
3) the seals, trumpets, and bowl judgments
4) the destruction of Babylon
5) the marriage of the Lamb
6) the war of the beast and the kings of the earth against Jesus and those who are the called, chosen, and faithful
7) the second coming of Christ to earth
8) the judgment of the nations
9) the millennial (1000-year) reign of Christ
10) the first resurrection
11) the binding of Satan in the bottomless pit
12) the release of Satan from the bottomless pit in order to deceive the nations
13) the battle of Gog and Magog
14) the great white throne judgment
15) the second death
16) the lake of fire (note who goes into it and when)
17) the new Heaven and new Earth
18) God wipes away all tears, no more sorrow or death

∽ When the angel showed John the bride, the wife of the Lamb, what did John see?

∾ What did you learn about the holy city, the new Jerusalem?

   a. How is it described?

   b. How is it illuminated?

   c. Where is its temple?

   d. Where does it come from?

   e. Who lives in the holy city?

   f. Who is allowed into it and who is not?

   g. What is the relationship of the nations to it?

   h. What is the relationship of the Father and the Son to this city?

∾ What did you learn about the tree of life in Revelation 22?

∾ How does the book of Revelation end?

   a. What parallels do you see between Revelation 1 and Revelation 22?

   b. What did you observe from marking every reference to *this book*?

   c. What words of exhortation are given to the reader?

   d. What warnings are given in this last chapter?

   e. What is the invitation that is given? To whom? What is the promise?

∾ What is the most significant thing that you learned as you studied the book of Revelation?

∾ How has this study affected you personally?

THOUGHT FOR THE WEEK

Without Revelation the Bible would not be complete. Revelation gives us "the rest of the story." What began in

Genesis is brought to completion in Revelation. What started out as defeat comes to ultimate triumph. Revelation shows us very clearly that God is God. He has never left His throne. The mystery of the seemingly prevailing force of evil is cleared up in Revelation as the mystery of God is finished and Jesus takes His throne and begins to reign upon the earth. Rightly so, justly so, the scroll is taken by the Lamb—He alone is worthy and able to break its seals. In righteousness He judges and wages war. At last, He is seen by all as King of kings and Lord of lords.

The enemies of God are made a footstool for Jesus' feet. When death, the last enemy, is conquered, the kingdom is turned over to God the Father. Finally, the tabernacle of God is among humanity! At long last God is seen by man face-to-face as He personally wipes away every tear from the eyes of those who are His beloved.

Then the desire and hope of the ages, the new Jerusalem, the holy city, prepared as a bride adorned for her husband descends from heaven. The bride needs nothing else; her heavenly bridegroom has prepared for her a home beyond her comprehension—a city that has no need of the sun or the moon for the glory of God has illumined it, and the lamp is the Lamb! None shall enter this city but those whose names are written in the Lamb's book of life. There will never be defilement or degradation of mankind again. There will be no more sin!

O Beloved, are you sure that your name is in the Lamb's book of life? Sure beyond a shadow of a doubt? If so, it is your responsibility to take what you have learned and share it with others—to bid them come and take the water of life without cost. It is also your responsibility to warn them of what the future holds if they refuse this gracious and merciful invitation of so great a salvation.

Don't add to the words of Revelation! Don't diminish them! You've been given a sacred trust. The words of the prophecy of this book are faithful and true; if you tamper with them, adding to or taking away from them you are setting yourself above God and then you will never sit in His presence. Your responsibility is to heed the words of the prophecy of this book.

So persevere, beloved and diligent student. Keep your garments white. Jesus is coming quickly and His reward is with Him to render to every person according to what he has done. There's a payday someday for the saints as well as for the sinners. Come, Lord Jesus . . . come!

	SEALS	TRUMPETS	BOWLS
1st			
2nd			
3rd			
4th			
5th			
6th			
7th			

Theme of Revelation:

SEGMENT DIVISIONS

Author:						CHAPTER THEMES
Date:						1
						2
Purpose:						3
						4
Key Words:						5
God						6
Jesus (Christ)						
in the Spirit						7
church(es)						8
throne						
mystery						9
repent						
overcome(s)						10
mark every						11
reference to						
Satan (demons,						12
devil, dragon)						
after these						13
things						
and I saw						14
(looked)						
angel(s)						15
seal(s)						
nations						16
trumpet(s)						17
bowl(s)						
plague(s)						18
wrath						
beast						19
Babylon						20
(woman)						
earthquake,						21
voices, thunder,						
lightning						22

NOTES

1. NIV: "what you have seen"
   KJV: "the things which thou hast seen"

2. NIV: "what is now"

3. NIV: "what will take place later"
   KJV: "the things which shall be hereafter"
   NKJV: "the things which will take place after this"

4. NIV: also *things, practices, ways, will, doing*
   KJV; NKJV: also *works*

5. KJV: *He that hath an ear*

6. KJV: *let him hear what the Spirit saith unto the churches*

7. KJV: *unto the angel of the church of . . . write*
   NKJV: *to the angel of the church of . . . write*

8. KJV: *To him that overcometh, He that overcometh*

9. KJV: "He that hath an ear, let him hear what the Spirit saith unto
   the churches"

10. NIV: also *things, practices, ways, will, doing*
    KJV; NKJV: *works*

11. NIV: *white clothes*
    KJV: *white raiment*

12. NIV: *white clothes*
    KJV: *white raiment*

13. NIV: *those who live on the earth*
    KJV: *them that dwell upon the earth*

14. NIV: *the earth and its inhabitants, (the) inhabitants of the earth*
    KJV: *the inhabiters of the earth, them which dwell therein, all that dwell
    upon the earth, the inhabitants of the earth, they that dwell on the earth*
    NKJV: *the inhabitants of the earth*

15. NIV; NKJV: "the hour of trial"
    KJV: "the hour of temptation"

16. NIV: *after this*
    KJV: *after this, hereafter*
    NKJV: also *after this*

17. NIV: *at once I was in the Spirit*

18. NIV; NKJV: *the scroll*

19. NIV: also *fury*

20. KJV: *voices*

21. NIV: also *thunders*
    KJV: also *thunders, thunderings*
    NKJV: also *thunderings*

22. KJV; NKJV: *lightnings*

23. NIV: also *nation(s), Gentiles, ages*
    KJV; NKJV: also *nations(s), Gentiles, saints*

24. NIV: *(attack, fought, battle, makes war)*
    KJV: *(fought, battle)*
    NKJV: *(fought, battle, makes war)*

25. NIV: *desert*

26. NIV: "when"
    NKJV: "now when"

27. NIV: *was hurled (down), had been hurled*
    KJV: *was cast (out)*
    NKJV: *was cast (out), had been cast*

28. NIV: *has been hurled down*
    KJV: *is cast down*
    NKJV: *has been cast down*

29. NIV: *the inhabitants of the earth, them, its inhabitants, all inhabitants of the earth*
    KJV: *them that dwell on the earth, them which dwell therein, all that dwell
    upon the earth*

30. NIV: *the image of the first beast, it, the image, an image in honor of the beast*

31. NIV: also *the great prostitute, the mother of prostitutes*
    KJV: also *the great whore, mighty city*

32. KJV: *vial(s)*

33. NIV: also *power to rule*

34. KJV; NKJV: also *wife*

35. NIV; KJV; NKJV; also *make war*

36. NIV: also *lake of burning sulfur*

37. NIV: *according to what they (he) had done*
    KJV: *according to their works*
    NKJV: *according to their (his) works*

38. NIV: *according to what they (he) had done*
    KJV: *according to their works*
    NKJV: *according to their (his) works*

39. KJV; NKJV: *works*

40. KJV; NKJV: also *the holy Jerusalem*

41. KJV: *that great city*
    NKJV: also *the great city*

42. NIV: *the fiery lake*
43. NIV; NKJV: *keep(s) the words*
    KJV: *keep(eth) the sayings*
44. KJV; NKJV: *the book of life*

Books in the
International Inductive Study Series

Teach Me Your Ways
Genesis, Exodus, Leviticus, Numbers, Deuteronomy

∾

Choosing Victory, Overcoming Defeat
Joshua, Judges, Ruth

∾

God's Blueprint for Bible Prophecy
Daniel

∾

The Holy Spirit Unleashed in You
Acts

∾

God's Answers for Relationships and Passions
1 & 2 Corinthians

∾

Free from Bondage God's Way
Galatians, Ephesians

∾

Behold, Jesus Is Coming!
Revelation

Also by Kay Arthur

How to Study Your Bible

Beloved

His Imprint, My Expression

My Savior, My Friend

God, Are You There

Lord, Teach Me to Pray in 28 Days

With an Everlasting Love

DISCOVER 4 YOURSELF!

iNDUCTiVE BiBLE STUDiES FOR KiDS

Bible study can be fun! Now kids can learn how to inductively study the Bible to discover for themselves what it says. Each book combines serious Bible study with memorable games, puzzles, and activities that reinforce biblical truth. Divided into short lessons, each individual study includes:

- a weekly memory verse
- Bible knowledge activities—puzzles, games, and discovery activities
- Optional crafts and projects to help kids practice what they've learned

Any young person who works through these studies will emerge with a richer appreciation for the Word of God and a deeper understanding of God's love and care.

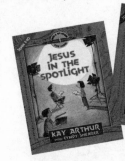

Kay Arthur and Cyndy Shearer
Kids "make" a movie to discover who Jesus is and His impact on their lives. Activities and 15-minute lessons make this study of John 1–10 great for all ages!
ISBN 0-7369-0119-1

Kay Arthur, Janna Arndt, Lisa Guest, and Cyndy Shearer
This book picks up where *Jesus in the Spotlight* leaves off: John 11–16. Kids join a movie team to bring the life of Jesus to the big screen in order to learn key truths about prayer, heaven, and Jesus.
ISBN 0-7369-0144-2

Kay Arthur and Janna Arndt
As "advice columnists," kids delve into the book of James to discover—and learn how to apply—the best answers for a variety of problems.
ISBN 0-7369-0148-5

Kay Arthur and Janna Arndt
This easy-to-use Bible study combines serious commitment to God's Word with illustrations and activities that reinforce biblical truth.
ISBN 0-7369-0362-3

Kay Arthur and Janna Arndt
Kids become archaeologists to uncover how God deals with sin, where different languages and nations came from, and what God's plan is for saving people (Genesis 3–11).
ISBN 0-7369-0374-7

Kay Arthur and Janna Arndt
Focusing on John 17–21, children become "directors" who must discover the details of Jesus' life to make a great movie. They also learn how to get the most out of reading their Bibles.
ISBN 0-7369-0546-4

Kay Arthur and Scoti Domeij
As "reporters," kids investigate Jonah's story and conduct interviews. Using puzzles and activities, these lessons highlight God's loving care and the importance of obedience.
ISBN 0-7369-0203-1

Kay Arthur and Janna Arndt
God's Amazing Creation covers Genesis 1–2—those awesome days when God created the stars, the world, the sea, the animals, and the very first people. Young explorers will go on an archaeological dig to discover truths for themselves!
ISBN 0-7369-0143-4